# LAMPS *and*
# LAMPSHADE
# MAKING

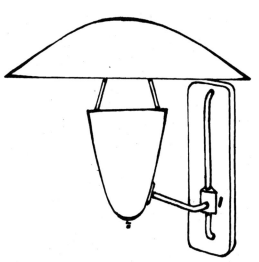

# S. PALESTRANT

*To Sarah . . .*

the guiding light and the lamp of wisdom in our home.

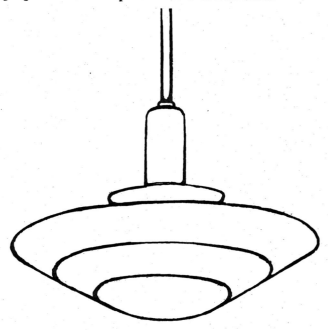

# Table of Contents

# *Foreword*

Before we can discuss lighting we must first understand the basis which gives rise to its need—illumination for vision. Without this, there is no special need for lighting and for lamps and no need for special lighting and lamps either.

We must accept certain premises as truisms. First, that everything we see is in the nature of color. Second, that we see things in relation one to another—not one thing at a time. Our concentration may be on just one thing, but we do see the surrounding objects too. Third, that peoples' vision do vary greatly.

Knowing these, we should reach certain conclusions about natural and artificial lighting. We must primarily think of lighting as a visual assistance from the point of foot-candle supply, secondly as a color source and last as an emotional stimulation which contributes to a mood.

When we talk of lighting, we mean artificial light, but do we not spend more than half of our waking hours in natural light—daylight? First, let us consider lighting from the approach of the home decorator and adjust to the visibility of things as we go along.

With the above in mind and to appreciate more thoroughly the problem of artificial lighting, it is necessary to understand what man-made light is expected to do. During the day, the sun is earth's incandescent lamp—its prime source of illumination. On a bright summer's day, direct sunlight supplies about 10,000 foot candles of light. A foot candle is the amount of light received from a candle one inch thick at a distance of one foot from its flame. Even in the shade of a tree one can measure about 1,000 foot candles. Normally, all other factors being equal, this should be good light, even for reading. However, on the average veranda one can expect to find but half of this light, about 500 foot candles, whereas at the same moment, just inside the house, at window position, it will measure as low as 100 to 200 foot candle power. At the very center of the average room, the same hour and day, one might get as low as a 2 to 10 foot candle readings. After sunset, the average house lamp too often supplies only about 5 foot candles of light to this artificial pool. It becomes necessary, therefore, to add lamps and lighting fixtures which will add more light directly from its bulbs or be built up with reflectors, echoes and any other means known and available.

The home decorator must realize that daylight is gathered into a room through windows acting as light traps. It is then distributed as needed by means of echoing light paths set up by the reflections received from mirrors, light hues and/or glossy wall surfaces and the cleverly conceived echo boxes lurking on the satins, metallic surfaces, polished woods or glass. Artificial illumination has the added advantage over daylight by being able to include as many sources of light as may be desired and distribute them as cleverly and judiciously as is possible.

Lighting serves several functions. Its prime purpose is to supply sufficient wattage to illuminate the area properly and best serve the purpose for which it was planned. Secondly, it should aid in carrying out the design and color scheme of the whole of the section of the room in which it plays its part. Finally, it should help to set the mood and visually aid in the emotional requirements set for the place it serves. In short, it serves as a visual element in preparing the attraction, the sustained interest and the basic needs of the room of which it is an integral part both functionally and decoratively.

# *Introduction*

General scientific research has come to the conclusion that lighting a room is not a matter of pouring into it a quantity of wattage which will flow like water and distribute itself adequately within it all by itself. It is revealed that two kinds of lighting are needed in any room, *specific* light leveled at the seeing task and *general* lighting which helps to avoid the eye strain and discomfort caused by being forced to look at strong contrasts between light and dark areas. This helps one to enjoy easier seeing through freedom from uncomfortable glare and to reduce the fatigue which accompanies it. Let us examine the structure of lighting more closely.

Lighting can be either *direct* or *indirect*. In the first case, the source of illumination is not obvious though its effects are seen and felt. Cove lighting, hidden "spots". black light, etc. are some examples of such where the results are of utmost importance. The means of achieving it must attract little or no attention to itself. In cases where the source of illumination is in obvious sight, it must become part of the decorative scheme and suitable in size, shape, texture and color. This becomes a decorator's problem.

The lamp has a physical appearance which must become an integral part of the decorative scheme like any chair, picture or the draperies. Because of its concentrated intensity of color—the light source itself—it must be played down to its proper importance or it may become the domineering part of the whole theme, whether it is so desired or not. It must, therefore, be considered that the lighting instrument, the lamp, is a unit of decoration besides a functional source. It must be planned to become a part of the group it serves.

To begin with, if we are seeking to light a room properly, we must be sure that sufficient foot candles or wattage of light is supplied for GENERAL ILLUMINATION. This must permit comfortable movement within all parts of the room and clear visibility of various groups of furniture and furnishings within it. This requirement is basic.

Now follows the SPECIFIC LIGHTING. Here the answers are not quite so simple, for each group requires a specific solution or solutions depending upon the complexity of the decorative questions posed. The amount of light source is based upon what the planned task is determined for that group. Is it reading, writing, televiewing or just conversation? Each demands a different specific wattage and in turn also affects the *general* or *key light*. Obviously, the key lighting for writing is much greater than what is needed for televiewing. There should rarely if ever be more than a ten per cent difference between the two—the key and the specific illumination. When there is, eye fatigue reaches its critical point more rapidly. Concentrated pools of light are excellent for hypnosis, but hardly good for effective work for any protracted period of time.

Whether this specific lighting is supplied from a source near at hand or beamed across indirectly to cover the area is immaterial. Strong shadows should be avoided unless they are designed to play their parts in the patterns of the room. Otherwise they are distractive and eventually annoying.

Another factor is whether this specific source is of high-level or low-level origin. People seated there must not be jarred by these strong pools of light glaring at them. It is disconcerting and attracts attention to the faulty design of the room. By the same token, neither should people who stand nearby or walk past a lamp be blinded by a raw blot of light jabbing at them.

Once these functional requisites are fully developed, the problem becomes one of lighting aesthetics. Are there sufficient lamps, etc. set about to create a tonal balance in the room? Are they keyed in relation to each other and to their individual tasks to create a visual rhythmic pattern? Do they attract attention to themselves and the groupings they serve out of relation to their importance in the room? Do they lead the guest from one to another ending with the center of interest of the entire room? Are they of the correct color and the correct amount of light? Do they enhance those things which they illuminate? Are they of the proper quality of intensity, field of influence and positioning to set and maintain the mood of their own groups, those within their orbit and within the room in general? These are basic questions and all must be cross-evaluated so that no facet suffers in the answers and all answers balance each other in the ratio of their achievements.

# Part I — Basic Illumination

# ℒamps in 𝒟ecoration

Lamp, by definition, is any piece of apparatus, constructed to contain some substance which will burn and result in illumination. Not considering the torch, the lamp showed strong evidence of its presence in the "festival of lamps" in temples during the earliest of Egyptian civilization, but not until about the year 4 B.C., did it become a household item of general need in Greece. The late Greek and Roman Age saw the lamp— a commonly accepted necessity—rate decoration and style of its own. They had their pendant lamps, some with multiple spouts. Sometimes, many lamps were grouped and hung in the center of the chambers. More often, they served as bracket lamps with a designated niche for them in each room. They served as portables, too, being carried when needed from one chamber to another and set near the person to permit him to "accomplish his tasks". Let us discard any discussion of the torch or lantern, although it was "lampas", the Greek name that was later used to describe all lamps but the torch. This type of mechanism, a wick floated on oil, was the lamplight of the world until replaced by the stearin candle which in itself meets that description, its "oil" being congealed in another form and consistency. The kerosene lamp was only a refinement of form and fuel, but in principle no different.

Modern invention of illuminating gas fixed the lamp terminals of these pipe conductors to preset positions in the room. Portables, such as table or floor lamps, remained of the oil-lamp age. It wasn't until the advent of commercial use of electricity in the late 19th Century that the lamp was freed from these fetters and permitted to roam the room as far as its wire could safely extend. From this point on, portables became more prominent and commanded individual attention because of its latitude of serviceability.

At first designers, bound by tradition, sought to electrify those existing pieces which lent themselves to such adaptation. Candlesticks and candleholders, vases, kerosene and oil lamps, small statuary, and even kitchen utensils were used. When they ran out of these, conscious efforts were made to manufacture and imitate such forms, regardless of their illuminating limitations. Not until the rebellion of the "Moderns" in the first decade of our 20th Century was there any deliberate break with such tradition in the attempt to design lamp fixtures from the functional approach. This was the birth of recognition of the engineer, the architect and the designer as well as the closer interrelationship of the arts and sciences for all home, architectural and industrial design. These partnerships produced incalculably new functional forms to serve every need and every occasion which was to remain with our civilization as the Modern Style. They even produced new illuminating means which, in turn, gave rise to a complete change in thought, purpose and to the resulting lamp forms. The end is not in view and its seems exciting to realize that during our life span, perhaps within our "sight", we may witness the birth and development of some remarkably new invention to take us further along this "light" road.

# Methods of Lighting

Lamp light requires as its fundamental impulse some source of current unless we refer to the candle, kerosene or illuminating gas lamps. These, while still used in some sections of the country where the supply of electricity is unavailable, present totally different problems and are in such minority demand that we shall ignore it here. For our purpose, an electric current is used to generate light by activating some type of lamp. Current is gotten from batteries or from a generator, either nearby or remote. In the case of the batteries, only *direct current* (DC) is available which means that the flow or the path of this current is in one direction only. Of course this current can be transformed to *alternating* (AC) *current* if desired. This type of current changes its direction of flow, up and then back. A common *frequency* of such alternation is 60 cycles per second. This means that the *voltage* which is the measure of electrical pressure changes its direction 60 times each second. It is common practice to speak of it as 60 cycles current. Of course there are generators which produce current of other alternating frequencies such as 45, 50, 35 or 75.

Direct current can also be produced by a generator, a mechanism designed to do this. To change DC current to AC current, alternators or rectifiers are connected with the wiring scheme somewhere between the DC source and the point of use intended for this type of transformed current.

Most electrical apparatus is designed to operate with both DC or AC. If not, the piece of mechanism will state which one it does require. Since practically all commercially supplied current is AC, it is just as well to regard all our current as such. Where it is otherwise important to use DC, it will be so noted somewhere in the directions or description of the object.

Light sources may supply illumination to a room and may remain visible itself as would a lamp bulb. This is called *"direct light"*. It may, however, be reflected from some surface away from its source. This is called *"indirect light"*. With the same amount of such light emanating, the

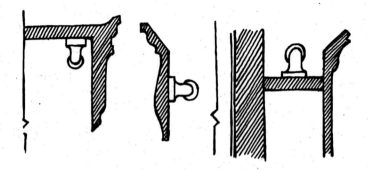

direct light would attract greater attention and will be stronger. The indirect light dissipates some of its illumination when the surfaces from which it is reflected absorbs a percentage of it. The darker and the duller such surfaces are, the more light is lost to its final point. Furthermore, indirect light must of necessity travel a longer distance than direct light and therefore expends a part of its energy and illumination enroute.

In room decoration both types of lighting are necessary. The indirect or concealed light serves to give more effective general, over-all illumination. The direct type produces the lighting accents in a group or within the room. It supplies illumination for specific needs. One type supplements the other.

Electric lamps are sources of radiant energy which produce the kind of wave length according to their intended use. Basically the spectrum covers a range of wave lengths commonly recognized by its three divisions. The infra-red area includes the longer waves which are emitted as heat, the middle group which produces light and is recognized by us as color and finally the shorter wave lengths in the ultra-violet region have special solar, germicidal and black light effects.

Such radiant energy may be passed along to heat up a solid or a gas until it glows in its own incandescence. Common among these are carbon or tungsten filaments and gases like nitrogen, argon, krypton, sodium, hydrogen, even mercury and neon.

In the *incandescent* type of lamp the electric current passes through its filament, heating it through a resistant-action until it glows as brightly as it can thus producing light. The greater this resistance, the greater its incandescence. However, with the fluorescent lamps, gas acts as the conductor of the electric charge instead of the filament. Light is produced by electronic activity rather than by heating an element.

In simple terms, the incandescent lamp consists of a glass bowl in which a filament, connected to terminals, sets up a resistance to electric current. The amount of such current consumed in passing through the resistant filament heats it to incandescence. This determines the voltage and wattage of the lamp bulb. On the other hand, a fluorescent lamp consists of a tubular bulb filled with argon gas and mercury vapor with an electrode sealed in each end of the bulb.

The tube is coated on the inside with a layer of fluorescent powder

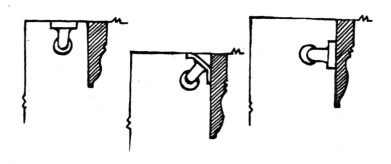

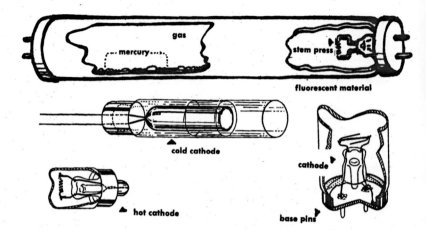

gas

mercury

stem press

fluorescent material

cold cathode

cathode

hot cathode

base pins

which absorbs the ultra-violet energy and transforms it into visible light. When proper voltage is applied to the electrodes, a flow of electrons is driven from one and attracted to the other. This flow of electrons through the mercury vapor results in the production of ultra-violet radiation which is then transformed to visible light. The amount of flow of electrons determines the amount of ultra-violet radiation; hence the visible light. Since any design of fluorescent lamp as to length, diameter or wattage requires a specific lamp wattage and current, it is necessary to wire a ballast into the circuit to deliver these essentials. The ballast must be properly specified for the circuit on which it functions, whereas the lamp remains the same for each condition. Starter switches are included so that a preheated current can flow through the filament cathode and heat the lamps momentarily. After a few seconds, the starter circuit automatically opens and the lamp lights. Different sizes of lamps necessitate different sized starters.

Since a lamp is only as good as its efficiency for its job, we must expect that lamps will vary in sizes, shapes and bulb finishes. Sizes are determined by the wattage they must consume to reach incandescence or maximum electronic flow. The higher the watt designated, the greater the amount of light should be expected.

Shape is determined by the particular part planned for the light bulb to play in the decorative scheme. This thought will be expanded on later. Incandescent lamp shapes are generally classified in ten groups and designated by letters shown in the accompanying lamp bulb chart. The fluorescent lamp is either straightline of varied diameters or circline.

Filament lamps of various lighting services have different types of bulb finishes. "Clear" lamps are generally satisfactory when used in enclosed diffusing equipment or shielded reflectors which protect the eyes from glare. The "inside frosted" gives added light diffusion and helps to eliminate striations and shadows. "Daylight" lamps are inside frosted or clear, having blue-green glass, thus producing a whiter, more color-corrected light. "Silvered bowl" lamps have a coating of mirrored silver on the bowl to form a shield and built in reflector particularly suited to types of indirect lighting equipment. Open type, direct lighting fixtures call for redirecting of about 80% of the light. "White bowl" lamps serve this purpose and help to soften shadows and reduce glare at the same time. "Enameled" lamps are well suited for general use and give a well-diffused

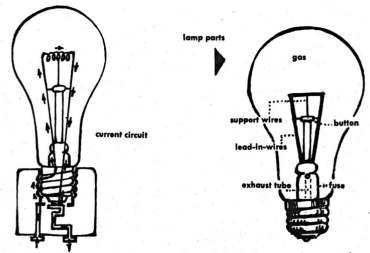

**lamp parts**

gas

current circuit

support wires ... button

lead-in-wires

exhaust tube ... fuse

light. They have the advantage over frosted bowls because they may be had in several colors. They also clean easily. "Colored and tinted" lamps are used for more specialized purposes where decorative effects are desired.

Fluorescent bulb finishes vary only as to their inside phosphor coatings, producing a diffused but spectrally different colored light. These are excellent when combined to produce tonal changes and mood control in room decoration.

There are many special purpose lamps each made to produce a wave length which will serve its particular need best. Some of these do not fit into any lighting scheme which a home decorator might use like the infra-red or the carbon arc lamp. The first affords only heat, whereas the latter produces an open flame incandescence which is too powerful for the confining limits of a home and far too much of a fire hazard. There are ultra-violet lamps which produce "black light". This light, while actually not seen, sends off rays which activate fluorescent objects or those coated with paint or other material having such properties. These lamps when directed toward certain objects cause them to glow and reveal their presence. Such lamps should, of course, be concealed from view. Their presence is important only in that they supply the necessary ultra-violet rays. They do not add any decorative value to the arrangement of things although that too may be achieved. Lamps such as the sodium or the mercury supply hard or intense light or both. Any of these factors are much too difficult to reduce in importance unless so much other light is added that the entire place moves up to a very high key in light and becomes overbright for normal living or for normal-sized quarters.

Light may be reflected, diffused and even bent around a corner. The former uses glossy surfaces which reflect light beams in such direction as are planned by the angles of reflection. Glaring pools of light may be softened or diffused by filter screens and lenses which break up these beams and softly "spill" them about. In both of these methods, some light is lost in the operation and the results are not as efficient as the expenditure of light at its source. However, light rays may be "piped" through a bar of plastic (lucite or plexiglas) to be bent around corners to illuminate the almost impossible places with little loss of light. This "bent light" may be used to decorative advantage by some ingenious and imaginative person.

|  | direct | semi-direct | general diffuse | indirect | semi-indirect |
|---|---|---|---|---|---|
| pendant style | | | | | |
| wall type | | | | | |
| table type | | | | | |
| floor lamp | | | | | |

# *Types of Illumination*

Just a word about the types of illumination is in order so that the reader can keep his terms, their special meanings, and their differences straight. It should help him to understand and to think around their similarities and their differences.

First there is the incandescent light. Illumination is caused when a current is passed through a lamp containing a filament which is heated to its point of incandescence. Sometimes the bowl of the lamp is pumped free of all gases so that the filament glows in a partial vacuum. There are other lamps which have special gases pumped into them to aid the incandescence in color and brilliance. All this illumination occurs within the visible range between the infra-red and the ultra-violet at the other end of the spectrum of visibility.

The infra-red rays are basically short-wave, heat rays which are not used directly for illumination. It is practically worthless from that point except to excite some material upon which it strikes and render it "visible" to special equipment like infra-red film.

The ultra-violet "light" is commonly called "cold" light. It comes from the long ray end of the spectrum. The more popular, commercial name for it is black light. These rays, like those at the opposite region of the spectral scale, emit ultra-violet radiation which excites certain materials causing them to glow and appear visible while this light is shining upon them. Such material rendered visible are called phosphorescent. This type of illumination has its greatest use in the decorative field or as a "novel" method of disclosing hazardous objects in the darkness. This is only one such use of black light.

Household and general purpose lamps range from 25 watts to 300 watts and are equipped with medium screw bases. Higher wattage lamps, 500 and up, intended for commercial and industrial lighting service have mogul bases. Lamps in sizes appropriate for either residential or commercial, such as the 300 watt size, are made in both medium screw bases, regular and skirted and in mogul screw bases. Mechanical strength and protection against overloading are important factors that determine the size of the base.

A brief explanation of how a base functions is this: One lead-in wire is soldered to the rim of the base, the other to the center contact. These parts are separated from each other by a glass insulator which appears as a black ring around the center contact.

**19**

# The "How and About" Lamps and Parts

## ABOUT WIRES

Basically, wires are either "solid" strand and of the diameter needed or a series of many thin wires and enough of them twisted into a "cable" of desired diameter. Since the flow of electricity follows the path along the surface of the wire, the resistance is in proportion to the relationship of the amount of current which flows along the wire and the area of surface it has available for that action. Resistance causes heat to be created in the conducting wire. Therefore, if the thickness of the wire is reduced, its corresponding circumferential surface is reduced. This compels the same amount of current to flow along that wire at the same rate and results in increased resistance and heat in the wire. If a heavier gauge of wire is used, it will offer more wire surface, reduce the resistance and consequently the heat created in that activity. Another way of supplying more wire surface over which the current may pass is to use many thin wires to which, cumulatively, will make up the original thickness of the wire. This will add many more surfaces to the same gauge and more "roads" over which the current can travel with greatly reduced resistance.

All electric wires are covered or insulated to prevent the current from escaping enroute. This escape is called "short-circuit". Another reason for insulating wires is to prevent those wires which may get warm—even hot—from burning off the insulating materials and exposing the wire to a possible "short".

Each job requires its own amount of current, consequently its own kind and thickness of wire. Then, too, with this it also requires the proper kind of insulation. This should explain why magnetic wire is of lighter gauge than lamp cord, and lamp cord lighter than heating appliance extension wires. This explains why the latter will require asbestos insulation while the former can be safe with only a coat of enamel covering.

Unless one is told what gauge he is getting when purchasing wire, it becomes necessary to measure the diameter of the bared wire. A circular wire gauge is the device used to determine this. The bare wire is measured by trying it in the numbered slots until the perfect fit is found. The holes behind the slots are not used for measuring. These numbers have equivalents in decimals of an inch. For instance, #6 gauge equals .162 inch, #16 gauge is .050 of an inch, #22 is .025 and #28 is .012.

The kind of insulation used depends, definitely, upon the kind, gauge and the use to which the wire will be put. Some wires are molded into their rubber or plastic insulation; others are threaded through their "spaghetti" base and have their cotton cover wrapped or woven around it. Obviously,

| 6 | 8 |
|---|---|
| .162 | .128 |
| 10 | 12 |
| .101 | .080 |
| 14 | 16 |
| .064 | .050 |
| 18 | 20 |
| .040 | .032 |
| 22 | 24 |
| .025 | .020 |
| 26 | 28 |
| .015 | .012 |

stranded or cable wires are more flexible and therefore less apt to break in handling.

Most commonly used for extension cords are #14 cable, rubber covered, parallel lamp cord or the same gauge twisted lamp or fixture wire. To conform to most city building code and fire law requirements, check for an Underwriters' bracelet label which is clamped around the wire every two or three feet certifying to the standard of the wire and its insulation with the name of the firm which guarantees it.

Other kinds of wires used for a variety of reasons are the asbestos-insulated, twisted heater cord, appliance lead wires, general purpose building wire, motion picture machine wire, radio hook-up wire, T.V. aerial wire, annunciator or bell wire, double-covered cotton magnetic wire, enamel-covered magnetic wire and remote control wire.

An average circuit connects wires in several places along its line. Good joints and splices are, therefore, of vital importance. It may result in considerable trouble if they are not made mechanically and electrically secure. If they are made so as to permit the wires to be worked back and forth, or not soldered properly, they will, due to the formation of a coating of film produced by oxidation, cause poor conductivity at the point where the conductors join. This, in turn, makes the circuits where these splices occur constantly inefficient and out of order. On the other hand, because of the high resistance at the point of a loose-fitting contact, these poorly constructed joints will cause abnormal heating and sparking. If near inflammable material, it will prove a fire hazard.

The requirements of the National Electrical Code relating to joints and splices specify that "conductors must be so spliced or joined as to be both mechanically and electrically secure prior to soldering." The joints must then be soldered to insure preservation, unless some form of approved splicing device is used. It "must then be covered with an insulation equal to that used on the conductors." These regulations refer only to light and power wiring and are not established in the Code requirements for the wiring of low-voltage signal systems which should not interest us in our needs of this book.

Joints and splices must be insulated properly to eliminate all possibility of crossed, grounded and/or short circuits caused by such faulty contacts. In order to comply with such insulation requirements, tape is most often used. Rubber-covered wires are wrapped with rubber tape about the thickness of the rubber insulation over which friction tape is used to make a covering equal to the thickness of the original wire. This is considered to be sufficient although an extra winding or two may sneak in.

The ends of many wires which carry current must be connected and disconnected—sometimes frequently. The simplest method is to make an open loop, bending the end of the wire with a long-nose or round-nose pliers in re-

peated, short bends until the loop is formed. Either slip the slightly open loop around the screw post then press it tightly together with the pliers, or solder the closed loop closed and slip it over the connecting post. In either case, tighten the binding post screw. When these wires are to be disconnected frequently or the wire is of the stranded variety which will fray with use or break off especially if the tip is tinned, then they are fitted with small metal pieces called *lugs* and *terminals* (see illustration). The end of the wire is connected to the lug by a wrapped tie-in, by soldering the end or by pinching the lug clamps over it. This will depend upon the kind of lug used although soldering can accompany each one of these methods.

When soldering tips or splices, use a copper-tipped soldering iron, either gas or electrically heated. Good results will be obtained if the metal is properly cleaned and a well-tinned soldering iron is used when hot enough to make the solder run. Choose the right flux for the job; resin flux is preferred. Apply the flux to the clean joint or splice, hold the hot copper underneath and in close contact with the parts to be soldered, then apply the solder from the top. The rising heat melts the solder which flows through the crevices and deposits the excess on the copper tip of the soldering iron.

There are many ways of making splices, each technique having its own advantages. Basically, the method of joining wires for joint, tap or splice is this. First "skin" the wire; the length of wire "skinned" and the place it is "stripped" will naturally depend upon the kind of splice, joint or tap and where along the wire it is made. Secondly, the cleaned, bare wires are crossed and twisted firmly together. Third, the splice is then soldered as previously described. Lastly, it is taped, first with rubber tape, then covered with friction tape.

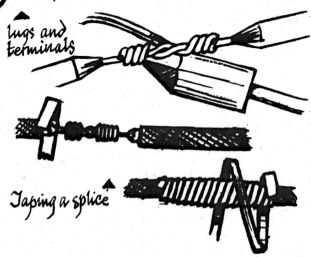

lugs and terminals

Taping a splice

22

Some of the more common splices are: 1) the Telegraph
Twist which is a long twisting of the wires, 2) the Western
Union Splice which has a telegraph twist ending on each
end with short, tight twists, 3) the Staggered Splice which
unites a double strand wire with the individual wires joined
about eight inches apart, 4) the Duplex Splice which is a
staggered, double wire splice using the Western Union tie,
5) the Flexible Wire Splice which is a square knot made
with stranded wire, the loose ends are twisted tightly about
the extended wire, 6) the Rat-Tail Splice which is made by
extending both ends in one direction and twisting them
together like a protruding tail, 7) the Terminal Fixture
Joint which begins like the Rat-Tail with one end extending
longer than the other, the long end wrapped around the
short one, then folded back, tied down by the longer one
and soldered, 8) the Through Fixture Joint which starts as
a Rat-Tail joint, and after a few twists one wire is bent
back to set them in a continuous line. The double ends are
then wrapped tightly around the returning wire, 9) the
Brittania Splice which is principally used on solid wires
rather than on stranded wires. They are bared and laid
alongside each other. They are then wrapped together with
"seizing wire." This is soldered and taped. 10) The Scarfed
Splice is another one used with the solid wire. The wires
are filed to a taper and laid alongside each other. They are
then wrapped tightly together with seizing wire. It is soldered and tape insulated. 11) The Multiple-Wrapped Cable
Splice is used more extensively on small stranded wires and
cables because it is pliable and may be wound together
without much difficulty. It is "skinned," cleaned and finger-
laced together as in the Ordinary-Wrapped Splice. The
strands of one are wound around the wire of the other in
one direction and the opposite group wound in the opposite
direction. Care should be taken that all strands in each

Knife

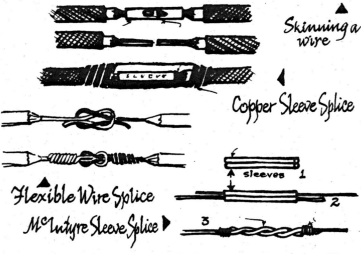

Skinning a
wire

Copper Sleeve Splice

Flexible Wire Splice

McIntyre Sleeve Splice ▶

sleeves   1

2

3

group are wrapped simultaneously and parallel to one another. 12) The Plain "TEE" Tap Splice is used to add a new lead to an existing wire without cutting the continuous line. One wire is wrapped tightly at right angles around a bared section of the line, then taped. 13) The Knotted Tap Splice is very much like the Plain "TEE" except that the first wrap goes around the back of the tapped-in wire and over its back to continue on the other side of this lead-in. It is finished like all the rest. 14) The Seizing-Wire Splice is used when cable or stranded wire is tapped into the line. One end of the wire is "stripped" bare and laid horizontally along the "skinned" section of the line wire, then wrapped with a one foot piece of #22 seizing wire. This wire is wrapped starting on the line, over a short piece of the insulation of the "lead-in" wire hugging both together tightly and continued on toward and over the bared end of this "lead-in." It may be soldered, but it must be insulated properly with tape. 15) The Ordinary Cross Tap Splice is just like the Plain "TEE" with two leads coming from opposite directions and at right angles to the main wire. It is finished in the same manner as the Plain "TEE." 16) The Elasticap Fixture Splice is a rubber cap used over a Fixture or a Rat-Tail joint splice. It saves taping and time. 17) The Sherman Connector is a small rectangular insulated tube into which a bared wire is inserted in each end, one from each lead and fixed firmly with a set screw. 18) The Bryant Solderless Connector is a plastic insulated cap into which the bared ends of the connecting wires are pushed. The cap is turned screw-wise and the copper coated, spiral spring insert acts like the threads of a nut and climb all over this "fixture joint." 19) The Copper Sleeve Splice is a copper tube which accepts the bared end of each wire into opposite openings. When inserted firmly, they are soldered permanently, then taped, 20) and the many threaded couplings which appear on the market from time to time under various trade names to serve as solderless splice and tap fittings.

## ABOUT SOCKETS

Following this line of description, we should then examine the various lamp sockets into which the "business" end of these wires eventually fit. The most usual of the household lampholders commonly called "sockets" are of the screw type variety in different sizes to fit the assorted lamp bases.

The largest of these in the incandescent group are respectively the Mogul socket, and the Three-Lite size. The Medium is the most commonly used; hence it is the most popular size. In the smaller division the Intermediate, the Candelabra and the Miniature run down the scale in that order. The special varieties rarely used in home lighting units except in the fluorescent or the special lamps are the Skirted, the Bayonet, the Disc, the Prefocus and the Bipin or Biposts. These are made in several basic materials like metal with fiber insulation, plastics and ceramics (porcelain).

Where the lamp switch is controlled by the wall or lamp base switch, the socket can remain Keyless. Otherwise the light switch must be incorporated within the socket utilizing as its switching mechanism the Key, the Pull-Chain or the Push button.

Fasten the wire in these sockets with *screw posts* around which the lead-in wires are bared and wrapped to be held in place by tightened screws, or *pin-teeth*, over which the wire ends are laid, insulation and all, which bite through the insulation, making contact with the bare wire within. Wires attached to the socket should be reinforced inside. Either the Underwriter's knot or the Friction Tape Tie is suggested. The former is tied into a square knot enveloping the wire (see diagrams). The latter is cross-taped with friction tape to spread the two lead-in wires to form a crotch. This tie holds the wires firmly in this position and keeps them from parting below this point. Should it become necessary to employ a male plug or caps at the other end of the extension cord, it is well to use the same method of reinforcing the wires there.

## ABOUT PLUGS

These Plugs or Caps have standard variations which we will list here. It cannot be a complete itemization since some of them would have no call for home or lamp requirements. We give you only the more popular and most commonly used. First, every cap makes its contact with its corresponding socket by means of poles, taps or prongs. The plugs may vary depending upon the circuit or appliance used. However, the straight *two-prong* plug set horizontally parallel is most frequently seen and used. A safety, non-slip cap uses the *twist-lock* variety. This shaped prong may be used on a plug with any number of prongs or poles. The two-prong variety may be set as *tandem-blades*, this makes another choice. When placed at right angles one to another, it is known as the *"Tee"* prong plug. Three blades curved to fit the circumference of the cap and placed equidistantly apart along it is called a *triple tap* plug. Besides the flat blades which are implied in those above mentioned caps, there is the *round pin prong*. Depending upon the polarity of the line, two, three, four or more poles will be used in the plug regardless of its shape.

correct

There are but a few methods by which the lead-in wires make contact with these prongs. The most commonly known are those which are wrapped around *screw-on* posts and tightened. Then there is the *pin-type* in which sharp pins in the cap pierce the wire insulation to make direct contact with the wire. Here the cap is tightened by screwing it down. It embeds the pins deeper into the wire and holds them firmly there. There is a cap which is cast directly over the wires and prongs. The contact is made first. Then the poles with their attaching wires are laid into a mould, *and cast* directly into a rubber or plastic body. Obviously, these cannot be replaced or rewired when removed. To overcome

incorrect

**25**

this shortcoming, a *snap-in* type of prong cap has reached the market. Here the cap is cast or moulded, but the prongs may be forced into position from the open end after the wires are twisted or soldered in place. It holds securely enough and since it is sufficiently simple to change, it has reached a degree of popularity among amateur electricians.

These caps come in the round or *standard* shape, regardless of the number of prongs, in narrow grip, in miniature size, in a square version of the round, as a rubber attachment or as polarity caps. Each has its use and its place. Of course the fluorescent lamp sockets have a different group arrangement since the structure of lamp differs from the incandescent kind. Here the lampholders are grouped in pairs, one pair for each lamp. These may be used as a single lampholder unit or combined to form multiple grouping. In any case the classification of one goes for all.

First, there are three methods of holding the lamp in its socket; with a rotating lock, with a spring mount or with a pin post—single or bipin. Using these holding devices, we then have several kinds of turrets or sockets. There is the single lamp unit, the twin turret or the triple turret. Then come others like the starter socket, the ejector type, the butt-on post, the narrow channel and the weatherproof type. Many of these come in standard, medium or miniature sizes.

## ABOUT OUTLETS

In conjunction with these sockets, outlets are necessary. These of the plug-in variety make their appearance in box covers, grade flash and one surface types. The wall flush kind are covered with a wall plate some of which have one advantage or another. These naturally are made to fit the style of switch used. Generally, they are: the tumbler type, the push-button switch, the convenient plug-outlets, the telephone outlet and the combination switch and outlet. Where one is needed to be covered, a blank plate is used to cover an unused spot, both to mark it and to keep it safe from hazard.

Since we mentioned switches, it is fitting that we mention the more common ones which appear on the scene. All of these naturally require switch plates to make them safe in handling. Here are some: the grade switch, the flush-tumbler, the locking switch, the pony-type switch, the dustproof, the heater, the panel switch and the knife switch. The latter is least likely to be seen since it is usually mounted on some surface and can hardly be adequately covered for safety. It is too clumsy to gain any popularity in the home. A dinner switch is one which rheostats its current through varying resistances to cause a lamp to burn brighter or duller. Other known switches sometimes used on a line cord or on a lamp appliance are the thru-cord switch and the single-pole canopy switch.

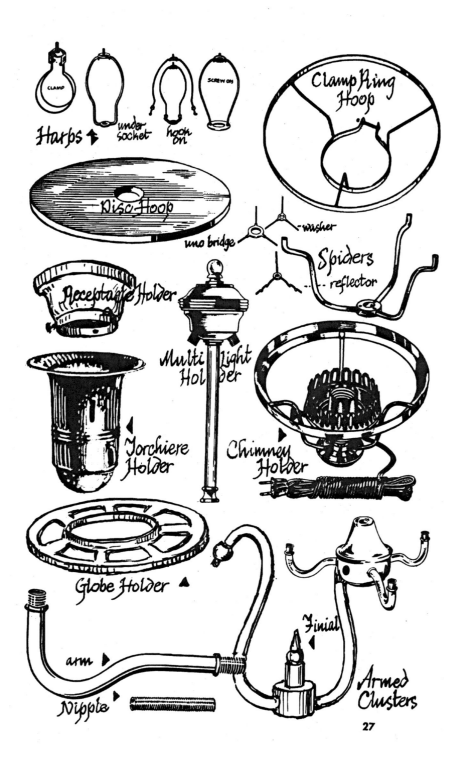

Harps
CLAMP
under socket
hook on
SCREW ON

Clamp Ring Hoop

Disc Hoop

uno bridge
washer
Spiders
reflector

Receptacle Holder

Multi Light Holder

Torchiere Holder

Chimney Holder

Globe Holder ▲

Finial ◄

arm ▶

Nipple ▶

Armed Clusters

27

## ABOUT LAMPS

We must not forget the most important single part of the lighting appliance—the lamp. Herein lies an entire field of study. Since lighting fixtures come in many shapes and serve their jobs from many positions, there must be a highly varied group to allow for the selection of the correct lamp for the job. Principally, the lamp must be made to take the kind of voltage which flows through the line. The most universally used are 110 to 120 for home use with 220 volts for commercial and factory distribution. Following this, lamps are made to glow at incandescence at watts reading from 2½ to 2000. Of course, the extreme ends of these readings are special lamps for special jobs. The home variety hovers around the average of 25 watt lamps to 200 watts.

As we realize, these lamps are asked to do different tasks. It is therefore recognizable that they will come in different bowl shapes. The most popular is an arbitrary shape which most nearly resembles a long-necked pear. Since it is most efficient to label such shapes, General Electric has published a listing with its accompanying code identification letters. The Arbitrary shape is called "A," "C" stands for a cone-shaped globe, "F" for the flame shape, "G" for the spherical or globe, "P" for the pear shape, "PS" for its variant—the straight-neck pear shape, "PAR" the parabolic, "R" is the

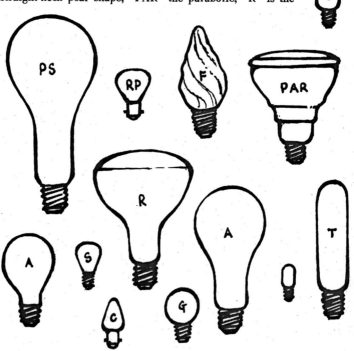

reflector bowl, "S" means straight sides, and "T" stands for the tubular type. Where the fluorescent lamp is involved they just fall into three classifications: 1) the general line lamp, 2) the slimline lamp, and 3) the circline.

To further aid in their tasks, these bowls are treated in many ways. There are those who have the inside frosted to diffuse the hard light, those which are frosted daylight (blue) to more nearly approximate normal daylight, those which are clear, transparent glass bowls and are most satisfactory for general lighting when enclosed in diffusing equipment or shielded reflectors to protect the eyes from glare. Then, too, there is the clear daylight which is intended to be used as the clear except that it offers a color correction towards approximately daylight. The white bowl is designed principally for use in an open type of lighting fixture. It diffuses and redirects the light. The silvered are lamps coated with mirrored silver to form a more highly reflecting surface. This may be silvered on the area around the neck or at the bottom of the bowl, depending upon where it is expected to reflect and in what position the lamp sets into its fixture. Sometimes they are semi-silvered to cause indirect lighting. The enameled lamps are general use lamps, diffusing and coloring the light since the enamel may come in white, blue, green and red. Colored or tinted lamps are sprayed on the outside and used in the highest lighting efficiency for decorative use.

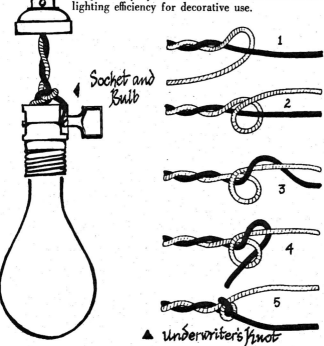

Socket and Bulb

1
2
3
4
5

▲ Underwriter's Knot

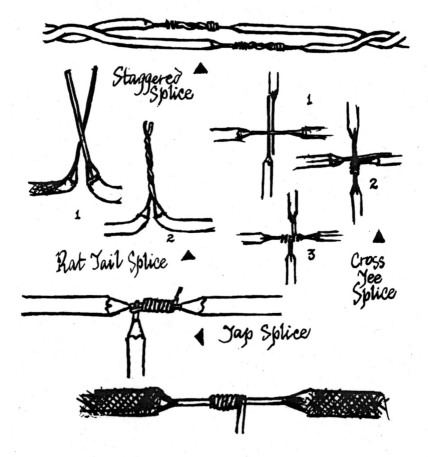

Staggered Splice ▲

Rat Tail Splice ▲

Cross Tee Splice ▲

◀ Tap Splice

Through Fixture Splice

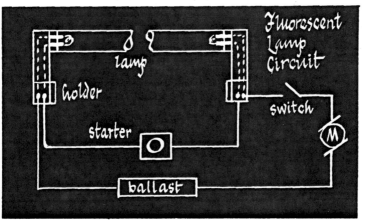

Fluorescent Lamp Circuit

lamp

holder

starter

switch

ballast

M

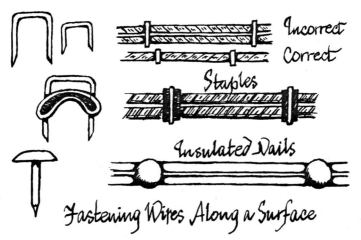

Incorrect
Correct

Staples

Insulated Nails

Fastening Wires Along a Surface

# Part II    The Lamp Base

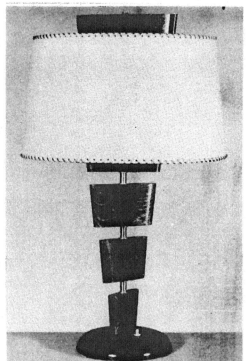

# Fundamental Lamp Groups

Basically there are but three major areas from which light may reach a room: the ceiling, the walls and from somewhere within the room itself by means of "portables". In all of these areas, lighting may be installed as recessed, flush, or extending fixtures. These lights fixture forms are determined by whether they intend to supply key or spot lighting. Then too, added factors are involved whether large areas are to be covered in one thrust of the beam and whether these beams are to be soft or hard light.

In the group called ceiling pieces, light may emanate from a ceiling fixture which casts its glow directly over the surrounding surfaces or from some nearby spot set to illuminate the ceiling. These are considered high level lights both in purpose and in plan.

Pendant pieces, like chandeliers, are used especially if the ceiling level is high. Light reflected from excessive distances loses much of its potential because the unused voids between soak up so much light to little or no purpose. These pendant fixtures make it possible to bring the source closer to the area of use with greatest of economy in output and efficiency. These lighting mechanisms should serve a decorative as well as a utilitarian purpose. Their shapes, materials and color must harmonize with the architecture and the interior decoration of the room.

Wall fixtures are devices which help bring illumination to the middle areas of the room. They serve as light balances and color controls in the decoration and are made in a variety of forms.

The most permanent of these are designed as part of the architectural scheme. These are disguised within the moldings and covered with baffles so that the light achieves a directional spill over predetermined areas of the room. Cove lights are one illustration of this type of lighting.

Strip lights judiciously placed in room corners and within window cornices illustrate another method of handling wall lights. Sometimes it may suit the scheme to maintain the same source of light after sundown as before. Lights thus embedded within the window frame or arranged to produce illumination from that direction, can continue the daylight design, functions and mood.

Shadow boxes and illuminated pictures aid considerably in establishing or heightening the mood of the decoration. They can be made to bring about the focal point in the design of a group within the room.

The wall fixtures do the same thing in a more direct manner. Here the mechanical structure of the light must be designed to be in harmony with the decoration, whether traditional or modern. Another variation of this, from a mechanical point and not from one of decoration, is to set the fixture against the wall to assume as much of the flat character of the wall and become as much a part of it as possible. Then again, it may project sufficiently to add the feeling of relief sculpture yet be kept attuned to the level of the wall expanse. Thirdly, it may extend to the point where it seems and is a lamp unto itself which merely joins the wall at some logical point of the lamp design. Lanterns, brackets, sconces, spots, clip-ons or pin-ups, swivels and gooseneck lamps fall into the classification of wall lights. Special conversions like binnacle or hurricane lamps, coach and carriage lanterns or kerosene and oil lamps are further possible applications of wall light fixtures.

Where wall lights cannot project sufficiently within the room design and where accents of light are necessary to the more mobile units of decoration, the portable lamp lighting group is required. These include floor and table lamps in every form, size and construction.

Based upon specific usage, lamps will require definite sizes and shapes which will offer the required output of illumination. Lamps intended for bed use must fulfill different requirements than those planned for the desk or for the reading chair. The general illumination and the specific area coverage vary greatly in the individual departments just as they do in any combination of purposes. Similarly, the vanity light differs from the study or work lamp or the closet fixture from the garden and lawn light. Their moods are many and their color and decorative requirements are individual.

The most transient of all lamp groups used in the home are the portables. These may be exchanged, replaced or removed for many reasons. Change of season, change of fashion, of taste, mood, change of accessories or furnishings—any of these may be reason for a change.

Prominent among these are the floor lamps which are so designed and constructed as to be an independent unit in itself. Extension cords make it possible to move them about and set them up in conjunction with a variety of furniture groups. These have taken many forms during the decades of traditional interior decoration and in their electrified form they changed very little. It is surprising how many variations of the torchiere floor lamp alone there has appeared within each era of home decoration. Add to that the reflector then the shade and you have innumerable elements added to the possibilities of combination and variation.

The smaller cousin to the floor lamp is the table model. These vary considerably in height. No matter how tall or short they might be, the overall height of the lamp and the object upon which it stands should add up to the overall height of a floor lamp—a height which permits a person to stand or set near it, whichever most suits the grouping, yet avoids having the lamp light strike the eyes directly. Thus we see a highboy and a desk lamp are both short while dresser and night stand lamps are made taller. End table and dressing table lamps are quite a good deal higher than the others only because they set upon lower pieces of furniture and their overall height must maintain a predetermined level.

Basically the lamp is made up of just three major sections: the base, the shaft, and the shade. Each of these sections may be comprised of one or more parts depending upon its function and the design of the lamp.

To begin with, the *shade* covers such parts as the shade, the reflector, the bulb, and the necessary accompanying hardware. The *base* includes the support, the clamp-on part and balancing pieces. These are determined by whether the lamp attaches itself to the ceiling, clings to the wall, rests on a table or stands on the floor's surface. The *shaft* is that part which joins the other two in either flexible or rigid "weldlock". This shaft may be long or short depending upon whether it must reach from table height or floor to eye level, above or below it. Additional parts added to its functions like swivels, extensions, telescoping arms, goosenecks, brackets, clip-on or counterweights are optional and are therefore added or omitted from the design and construction of the lamp as required.

Lamp design follows one of two trains of creative planning. It is either devised to fit the limitations of traditional periods of decoration or the problem is approached from the pure functional angle and it parts company completely with the period styles.

Very often "Traditional-Modern" is spoken of as an arbitration between both style groups. This appeasement is hardly feasible since "Traditional" approaches the problem from the point of decorative treatment, whereas "Modern" solves its problems functionally and stops right there.

To carry either one beyond its own conventional limitations, is to make mockery of the essence of the purpose and of the point of approach. Its mongreloid results can only be labeled by approximation in appearances, not by any functional period approach to lamp design which requires the limitation set upon the forms and materials employed used during that era and adapted to the electrification of present day technology.

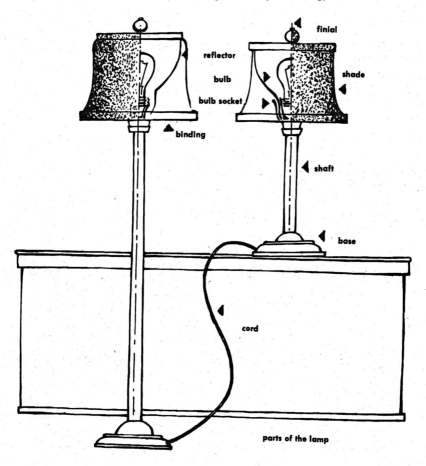

parts of the lamp

# Methods of Wiring, Tying, Binding

We know that a circuit is the complete route which current must travel from its source to the mechanism which it must feed. This route is delineated with wires which carry the current to its destination. Most commonly the seat of such current is an outlet of some type into which an extension wire is plugged to continue the path of the current to the lamp light itself.

Often, intervening between the source and the ultimate point of use, electrical devices are installed for special reasons. Sometimes, they are switches, sometimes fuses, sometimes rheostats or dimmers may be another outlet for a minor circuit.

These are double wires and each made up preferably of the multiple strand rather than the single wire variety. Each wire must be insulated. This will vary with the purpose of each kind of wire. Electric lamp wire will carry a smaller load than will a heating unit. Hence, a light—perhaps cotton insulation is necessary for the lamp while the heating cord requires an asbestos wrapping for its protection.

The average length of wire appendages which are attached to a portable lamp are about ten to fifteen feet long. These only vary with the exception. Extension wire longer than that shouldn't be necessary. An outlet nearer to the source is preferable. Extension wires should not be too long either. It presents a safety hazard and should be shortened to have only as much slack as is normally required to move the lamp to all sections of its own grouping. Otherwise it should be plugged into an outlet closer to the group.

All electric currents are basically alike. They only vary in the way they flow through the line. For instance, a continuous flow in which the direction is constant and does not vary in its amount of flow at any given instant is called CONTINUOUS CURRENT, whereas a similar current moving in one direction but whose current strength rises and falls, is known as a PULSATING CURRENT. Actually, any current created by a

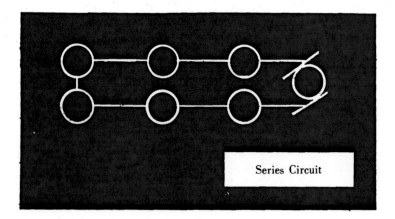

Series Circuit

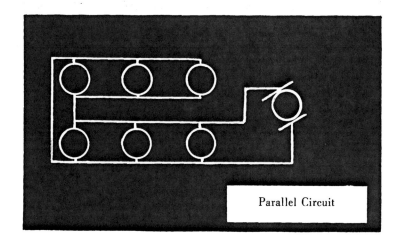

Parallel Circuit

generator is pulsating, but one which flows in a steady direction is known as DC CURRENT, but one which produces an electric current in which the flow reverses itself at fixed intervals is called AC CURRENT. OSCIL-LATING CURRENT is another form of AC current in which the flow diminishes from its maximum strength until it stops entirely. The frequency of such rise and fall of the flow is inconceivably big, often running into millions of complete oscillations each second. This varies from the INTERRUPTED CURRENT in which the circuit itself is made and broken at given and steady intervals. This type of current is used for sign flashers.

100 volts approximates one ampere charge, hence each 100 watt lamp takes about 1 ampere. Thickness of wire is measured in gage. Solid wire is very apt to break with much handling; stranded wire can withstand a great deal more. An electric current is produced either mechanically as in a generator or chemically as in a wet or a dry cell battery.

When a current passes through wires and pieces of electrical apparatus which are so connected that the current must move from one to another in turn, it is said to be wired in *series*. If, however, such current is divided two or more branches and passes through all of these at the same time, this is said to be set up in *parallel*.

In a Series Circuit, the current remains the same at each point in the circuit. Each lamp receives as great a charge as every other lamp. However, if one lamp is removed, the current is prevented from continuing through and the circuit is considered broken. In the Parallel Circuit, each branch of the circuit receives such part of the total current delivered to the combination as it needs for its function. The sum of these minor currents must equal the total current delivered. No unused portion can be stored. The excess will merely be distributed to all branches and may overcharge or burn out the electrical mechanism.

Unlike the flow of water, the flow of electricity demands a closed path. This path travels from its source of generation to its point of use and back again. It is to be assumed throughout that this flow moves in the direction from the positive ( + ) terminal of the battery or the generator back to the negative (—) terminal.

**37**

# Lamp Styles in Review

From the time the cave man carried a burning faggot and lit a fire on the floor in the center of his cave domicile to a period quite recent in our growth of civilization, there was no way of making light anything but a *point* of illumination. As these faggots became oil torches, candle sconces, then gas jets, they still remained single points of brilliance which radiated more or less light depending upon the ingenuity of the pattern arrangements of reflecting surfaces surrounding it. Similarly, the central lighting fixture which was the 17th Century's contribution to diffused lighting was a concentration of a great many candles hung in the middle of the room on a tremendous fixture. As a source of illumination it was more efficient than the wall bracket since the center of the room is much more the center of man's activity than the walls. The detached lamp, an offspring of the portable torch of old, is today an infinitely better lighting solution because its position as a light source may fulfill the requirements dictated to it by its associated furniture. Its very portability enhances its flexibility and scope of usage.

Reviewing the efforts of the designers and craftsmen of the past should help us to determine to a great extent basic lines, units of design, motifs and techniques of decoration, typical materials and generally accepted lamp pieces commonly used in the Traditional Periods of the past. But this can easily be used as a guide for the present selection.

The most important movements of furniture and furnishing was developed in just a few of the eminent countries of the world. The others either imitated or adapted these forms for their own convenience and taste. England, France and America were among the more important of these. At certain periods of civilized history, Spain, Italy, the Dutch and others made their mark felt.

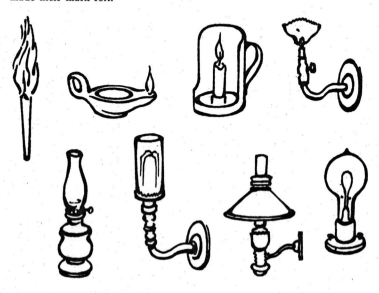

The attributed dates are generally very arbitrary, for styles of decoration are born long before they attain the recognition of maturity and continue to exist long after their loss of pre-eminence and the dateline of their official obituary. National and political boundaries are hardly a guarantee of the physical limits of a style. Often, there exist many cross-influences which tend to ignore man-made borders and devious routes of contact which defy any restricting enclosures. The year, 1925, marks the approximate, official beginning of the "Modern Style". Because of the strong, geometric cross-influences and imitations, it resulted more as an *international* style than a *national* one.

A history of lamp styles, as we now know it, is practically non-existent before the advent of the electric light in 1887, unless we stretch the definition of the word "lamp" to include all forms of illumination like the oil lamp, the candle and the incandescent gas mantle. Under this set of circumstances, it is virtually impossible to obtain an authentic period, electric lamp. The closest one can hope to get is an adaptation of some piece which may be closely allied to some preconceived notion of what an electric lamp should have looked like in that period of design or adapt and convert a standard piece of period accessory to serve as a "period lamp". All of this would normally fall under the heading of the Traditional Style.

In direct opposition to this philosophy of Lamp Decoration lies the Functional Modern with transitional group which grew out of the half-way thinking. The International Exposition of Decorative Arts in 1925 evoked tremendous interest in the various schools of design operating in Europe. The tendency ran in two schools; one, designated as the Romantic offering handsomely conceived forms strongly reminiscent of traditional forms, now developed into the "Traditional Modern"; the other, a social-engineering concept based upon "form which follows function", now recognized as the "Functional Modern". The latter was a natural out-growth of the social, economic and ideological changes brought about by our rapid 20th Century scientific development and technological growth. New materials and new techniques brought about new horizons. The fundamental concept of good materials, honestly expressed with fine craftsmanship of undisguised form influenced by function, stood out above all poetic obscurantism. This feeling spread throughout the continent, enveloped world art thought, and developed nationalistic trends along the way. It was based uniformly upon the naturalistic approach rather than stemming from the classical. The Bauhaus schools of Europe were vital factors in crystallizing artistic thought in this new direction.

In America, we still clung to the Traditional styles, sparked by manu-facturer to copy, and unskillfully at that, of the major historical styles with their misadapted historical motifs. Not until such iconoclasts as Louis Sullivan and Frank Lloyd Wright showed the amazing potentialities of the new age of steel, did we recognize this new external expression to have grown to adult size and importance. Not until two decades have passed have we given them the recognition due them, for at that time the commercial classicism was far too strongly entrenched. It took this length of time for homes to change in architectural function to require functional furniture and furnishings. It also took several world wars and their sub-sequent reconstruction to knit these world-wide elements into a universal style.

The simple, undecorated utilitarian form is adequately beautiful, if designed with an honest respect for the materials and the new conveniences that have come to serve our needs. In accordance with these special condi-tions, it becomes the logical conclusion that we design these implements of our everyday use to serve us best under those conditions. So too, does lighting by electricity create new problems and expose new possibilities. We should, therefore, wisely discard the technique of lighting by "elec-trified-candles and kerosene" and redesign according to these new ideas and possibilities. Thus the nature of the materials have become far more important than the designer's attempt at creating an aesthetic form in the established sense. The basic sense of beauty is achieved when the objects are designed precisely to their required use, their final forms being no more than the expression of this use and of the natural possibilities of the materials of which they are made. Non-essential ornament is dropped off like over-ripe apples.

Rooms cease to be regarded as the interior of a box. They are, rather, treated backgrounds and continuities of precise and enclosed activities. The furniture becomes more closely integrated with the walls, floors, ceil-ings, etc. Artificial lighting, ventilation, seating, sleeping, movements, eating and other elements of human occupancy become essential factors for artistic-functional conception and decoration.

# Materials for the Lamp Base

In the strictest sense of the word, there is no such thing as any one or another material most suitable for use as a lamp base. Almost any one material or combination of materials may be used. It depends for the most part on what form that material takes and to what purpose it is put. One may be more suitable from the point of view of texture, another from the standpoint of weight, a third may be more desirable for its color or even its strength. Material for the lamp base is chosen for its functional suitability, its physical and mechanical adaptability to supply the lamp needs, and for its aesthetic affinity to the style for which it is planned and the group in which it is expected to fit. These are the interlocking and overlapping areas which will determine the selection.

Even with this guide in view, one may arrive at several equally good selections. Personal taste is then an obvious factor. Involved with this is the limitation of materials called for by some who wish to adhere strictly to a particular traditional style and the possible availability of that material imposed by economic or geographic limitations. Let us scan the more common materials likely to be available and examine the varied forms in which they may be procurable.

First, there are the *ceramic* materials. These may vary from the rough, unglazed brick-like clays to the very delicate porcelains. There are many different kinds of clays, each, when fired, producing a different kind of "biscuit"—different in color, different in texture, different in strength. These may be glazed in many ways, the colors of the glazes depending upon the location of manufacture, place of import of glazing materials, and the technique used. These have been known to differ within the same locality in England, Germany, Italy or France because one locality may import its technicians or materials while the other utilizes its local talent.

To further complicate such choice, these same materials, techniques and craftsmen may produce a variety of forms, all adaptable to lamp base use. Statuary, pottery, geometric blocks and tiles are all possibilities as lamp bases; size, form, color and finish will determine to which purpose or place it is applicable. This material may require the addition of a base plate or some other device to add greater weight to secure stability for the lamp.

The choice of *wood* exposes a new realm of materials suitable for lamp base use. Here, too, the form will determine to a large extent, the kind of wood to be selected and the method by which it should be made. Suppose we choose solid wood planks. Geometric forms may be hewn from one relatively heavy piece of wood or else built up by assembling several thinner boards to construct the plinth, box or sphere. Full sculptural pieces will naturally require solid blocks of wood, whereas low-relief carving may employ pieces of lesser thickness. Piercing, underlays and even marquetry appliques may easily be used on thin panelling. Veneers are used mainly when an entire flat surface is to be covered with a thin film of wood to improve its color, grain and/or texture. Space forbids a complete explanation on the nature, types and techniques of woods. Suffice to say that a lamp base must have sufficient bulk to support the upper structure which is, of course, an integral part of the lamp itself.

*Metal* offers a variety of forms to the lamp base designer. While one metal may weigh more than another, be of a different color than the other, they are all manufactured in many similar forms. They come in sheets of assorted thicknesses (gauges) and sizes; as tubes of all diameters with a variety of wall thickness; as wire of all shapes like round, half-round, square, hexagonal, etc., and in many gauge thicknesses; as rods of the wire shape, but over one-quarter inch in diameter; of screening mesh woven from wire; as blocks and ingots from which castings are made; as special forms preshaped in the punch press or the stamping machine. These are only the raw forms in which they may be purchased to be worked on. Since metals differ chemically, they are bound to have physical properties which are more desirable for one reason or another. Color may vary, weights of metals are not alike, tensile strength, malleability, costs and working properties differ to such an extent as to make one metal more desirable than another for use in a particular lamp.

Some metals tarnish, covering the metal surface with a mellow color. Some receive coatings which are undesirable. These are the "patina" coloring which may be achieved either in due time and exposure, or may be hurried along by chemical persuasion. Techniques like anodizing of aluminum, metal plating, of one metal over the base of another to improve the whole or part of the surface for practical or aesthetic reasons, fall under the same type of technique as patina coloring.

In addition, the methods of adding surface decoration runs the whole gamut of metal techniques invented by man through the centuries. Etching, engraving, damascening, chasing, soldered or brazed appliques, enameling, piercing, stamping, punching, riveting, lapidary and the vast variety of abrasive finishes are just some of the decorative means at the craftsman's call with which to work on metal.

*Plastic,* the most recently popularized material, serves as a very adequate source from which to select and construct lamp bases. This material has distinctly individual properties, yet within its own sphere may vary greatly one from the other. All "plastics" are not alike, neither in color, weight, tensile or ductile strength, insulation and conductivity properties, nor in workability. In the main, all plastics fall into two basic divisions, the thermoset and the thermoplast, the latter of which covers most of our synthetic plastics. The *thermoset* group are those plastic materials which, in their process of manufacture, have been "fixed" and hardened by means

of heat and like scrambled eggs once fried, no amount of additional heat will cause them to soften. While the *thermoplast* materials, on the other hand, can be brought to a solid state with the addition of heat, can be re-softened later by the addition of "wet or dry" heat, whichever it may require.

These plastic materials are manufactured in many forms; sheets, rods, tubes, bars, film, fibers and extruded forms of the molding stripe. Whether fashioned from one piece or fabricated out of many, plastic lamp bases have to overcome their lack of weight which is so desirable toward the stability of a lamp.

There are in addition, the powdered and liquid forms of plastics which may be cast like plaster and "cured or set" under special conditions. This material ranges from the transparent kind, colorless or stained, in which various things may be embedded, to the full opaque kind, white or colored, which may be used in every way plaster of paris can, with the added advantage of having a harder, tougher material which can be polished to a much higher gloss. With this, preformed parts are possible as are decorative sculptured cap and base pieces, incised or low-relief modelled switch plates, etc.

The classifications of *rock*, more commonly accepted as stone by the layman, offers the lamp base maker a vast number of different materials which may be turned to advantage. In the *igneous rock* group we find the large family of granites so very popular with stone sculptors. Without involved detail, we can readily see that large, simple lamp bases easily adaptable to geometric or carved forms, are conceivably constructed from this type of material. There is no doubt that the stone-carving technique involved in this is a slow, painstaking process, but the end result is without any doubt a strong, durable and attractive lamp. The granite is available in many tones in the gray and tan families sprinkled with assorted colors of many minerals and ranging from a finely dispersed grain to a rather heavy sand-like effect. These may be polished to a very high luster or left matt-finished. The finest examples may be seen on tombstones. Then, of course, there is the volcanic glass, the obsidian, so popular with the Egyptian sculptors.

The *metamorphic rock* includes, in the main, the marble and the sandstone groups, the more popular of the two being the first. This runs the spectral gamut of white, cream-colored, the green, the gray and the red families. Adding to their beauty and interest, they come in the fairly uniform colors and range through the variated and veined markings. Marble can be polished to an exceedingly high luster. Some, like alabaster, are soft enough to be turned on a lathe. Softer still are the soapstones which can practically be whittled with a knife. These are available in tones of gray and in white highly tinted. Some have streaks and markings closely resembling their harder cousins, the marbles. These make interesting lamp bases.

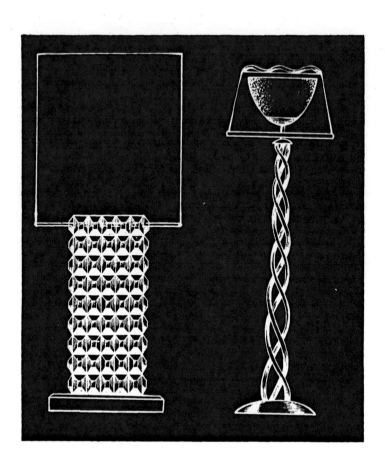

| METAL | | | |
|---|---|---|---|
| **BASIC AVAILABLE SHAPES** | **FORMING METHODS** | **DECORATIVE TECHNIQUES** | **FINISHING METHODS** |
| Sheet<br>Rod<br>Bars<br>Ingots<br>Tubes<br>Cast forms<br>Pressed or stamped<br>  preforms<br>Wire | Hammering<br>Sawing<br>Filing<br>Bending<br>Cutting<br>Drilling<br>Machining<br>Casting<br>Grinding<br>Soldering<br>Brazing<br>Welding<br>Riveting | Anodizing  Repoussé<br>Planishing  Damascene<br>Piercing  Plating<br>Chasing  Enameling<br>Soldering  Stipling<br>Riveting  Punching<br>Engraving  Stamping<br>Etching  Inlaying | Polishing<br>Buffing<br>Antiquing<br>Matting<br>Texturing<br>Lacquering<br>Waxing |

The *sedimentary* family of *rocks* provides us with the limestones and the soap stones in a variety of reds, tans and grays for the latter and in a range from white to black for the former.

In a limited selection, the *quartz* and *crystal* group may be adapted to use in the lamp base. Because these minerals are in the gem classification, they, obviously, come in smaller pieces, are of rarer vintage and certainly more expensive. The Orientals used these minerals with judicious taste as inlays or as small, sculptured medallions applied to other materials. Polish and luster are an important part of the attraction of these gem materials. There are examples of urns, vases and statuary pieces made of quartz and crystal made during past eras which have the potentiality and promise of comfortable conversion into lamp bases.

While dwelling on the stone products, it might be well to examine the materials closely resembling this group, the plasters and the cements. *Plaster of Paris* is a white, flour-like material which, when mixed with water hardens into a smooth solid mass. This may be cast into a mold of any pre-desired shape or formed into a conveniently sized block, then carved, whittled, filed or scraped into some form fitted as a lamp base. Plaster of Paris is basically white, but may be tinted or strongly colored with the addition of dry pigment or water paint during the plaster mixing process.

To overcome its surface softness and brittleness, it may be impregnated with a plastic material used for that purpose—Plaspreg. This has its limitations in that its color is then limited to a tan, a light brown or a mahogany blackish-brown. In the light tan process, color pigments added might help to supply some desired color. However, that color must of necessity be limited by a tannish overtone. Keene cement, which is "spent plaster" offers the greatest potentialities for interesting results in that field.

Other cements, of the more common outdoor variety, offer limited results of texture and limited colors of grayish cast. Its very character suggests larger and coarser forms. It does compensate by supplying stronger body materials.

*Glass* is very versatile and should not be overlooked nor underestimated as a lamp base material. Many fabricated forms such as glass, brick, heavy opal and marbleized glass plate and variegated plate glass are commercially available and can be fabricated or adapted to serve as lamp base forms. Then, too, there are many complicated forms which have been factory cast, blown or ground like statuary replicas, assorted and interesting bottles and glass balls and blocks which can be made to serve that purpose. Much of the sheet glass can be cut to size and, if of the right glass, be heated and bent to shape.

Decoratively, glass has a wide latitude too. It may be faceted and polished to gem-like reflection and serve as cut-glass. It may be decorated in two tones; polished and clear, against dull and gray. There are several

methods of accomplishing this. Gray carving with a grinding wheel is one, etching with hydrogen fluoride another, and wearing off the polished surface with emery dust blasting a third. When such glass is converted into a mirror, the surfaces become multiply attractive because of the colorful reflections it adds. Such mirrors may be of silver, gold or bronze coloration, whichever is preferred. While this is accomplished by plating the metal on the underside of the glass, it can look vastly different when plated on the front surface. This can be controlled to cover restricted or designated areas. Colored enamel paints may be used as an overlay like plating. This, however, is more likely to chip off, but it does add the entire scope of color for tone and design.

We are prone to overlook the use of *paper* as a purposeful material. When shredded into a pulp-like material, prepared for and cast into a mold or modeled, it becomes as useful as wood. What it lacks in grain and texture, it makes up in its flexibility and adaptability. Sheets of paper of interesting design and special textures may be laminated as veneers over other materials. Heavier cardboards may be cut and fabricated much like wood or sheet plastic material can function equally as well. It can be made into very rigid, strong, and durable bases, to stand up to constant, hard usage and show as little wear as most of its contemporary materials. By impregnation with plastics, plaster of Paris, gums like shellac, varnish and lacquers, paint and others, too numerous to mention. The advantageous part of using this material is that it may be decorated with all the techniques used on paper of all kinds, on wood, some of those employed on plastics when impregnated with it. It may be electroplated or coated with metal-leaf to resemble that material. Paper also has the versatility of assuming molded forms when it is mached over some sculptured surface or modelled out of paper pulp. Duplication of lamp parts or decorative units are entirely feasible by casting replicas out of the pulp material. Where the lamp requires greater stability, it can be acquired by properly designing it with a low center of gravity or by weighting the base.

Another very popular and decorative medium for lamps is *leather*. Since it can only be produced in sheet or film form, it can hardly become a structural material for the lamp base. It makes, however, very excellent cover-over surface decoration. The entire field of color and a vast coverage of textural qualities can be gotten from leather. This runs from the hairy hide with its identifying textures to the characteristic skin grains peculiar to each individual kind of leather. In some cases the leather is accepted for its inherent beauty of tone and texture, but some leathers may be further enhanced with added design. General or spot dyeing and painting seems an obvious method of treating the leather. Most of these techniques involve brushing the coloring matter on pre-planned places to create illustrative or formalized decoration.

Where strong color and pattern might become the goal and painting it on not desired, piercing or punching these designs and backing them

up with contrasting leathers can fill the requirement. Overlays or paste-on units pattern is an excellent alternate for piercing. In either method you get a low-relief or carved effect. Use a rubber based cement to unite the many smaller pieces to each other and to its background.

Should such strong effects be out of place, leather tooling can be substituted. Not all leathers can be accommodated to this application of surface decoration. Tooling is a form of low relief modeling of the leather, pressing some areas down flatter than others with a hard tool. This is sometimes called "blind tooling." Where metal-leaf is pressed into the design, it is referred to as "gold-leaf," "silver-leaf," "bronze-leaf," "aluminum-leaf," etc., designs.

A variation of pressing the design into the leather is to burn it in with very warm or a hot marking or stamping tool. This instrument might be heated over an open flame or might be a self-heating or electrified tool much like the common soldering iron with its tip shaped to some desired form. This, too, may be done "blind" or with "metal-leaf."

A protective covering of leather lacquer, varnish, even rubbed oil or wax is advocated to preserve the leather surface against dirt, abrasion, marring and general deterioration of time and atmospheric changes. This permits handling the leather in the normal routine of use and household care of cleaning.

Perhaps the largest and certainly the most common method of creating bases is by *converting* various items like vases, urns, candlesticks, figurines, canisters, sconces, kerosene lamps and so forth. There is no limitation to this type of lamp base. Here, the size of the object chosen to serve becomes the controlling factor in selecting the lampshade and all other decorative elements. Of course, the choice of such "base object" made, in the first place, has probably been made on the basis of fitness of form, decoration and color. Where one of these elements is inadequate, it may be corrected. Such applied therapy as might be required when converting a canister may involve a new paint job to hide the commercial appearance, its advertising and other "tags." It may require a veneer of other material such as linoleum marquetry, paper montage, glass veneering, textile upholstery, metallic facading, plastic pasteovers, etc. Some of these convertibles are adaptable entoto, others require subtraction, addition or combination with other forms. This is especially true when the selected piece is too large for its intended use or when too small. In the latter case, one may use two such items like two glass blocks or combine it with some mated or compatible object. The big problem then becomes a matter of technical solution—how to tie these together without damage and without attracting attention to the means rather than the forms themselves.

The range of choice for such lamp bases are legion and each suggests its own and varied means of adaption and decoration. The field is wide open.

# Part III  Lampshades

# Function of the Lampshade

When planning for a suitable and efficient lampshade, many problems must be solved from a functional and aesthetic point of view. The lampshade must be designed and engineered to include the best size and shape of the shade to do the job intended, the right materials to serve this job, the correct construction methods to fabricate this lampshade, and the most aesthetic decorative ideas and appropriate techniques to help beautify it.

Suppose a strong source of illumination is required from a lamp in question. Suppose, too, that this lamp is in such position within its group as to make it uncomfortable physically and aesthetically to sit within its glare. It, then, becomes necessary to shield that light from direct vision among other factors. While there are many possibilities of solution, the most obvious is to use a lampshade made of opaque material. This will break the direct line of the light rays and scatter them about to be redirected.

Very often louvres are used for this purpose. These are opaque strips which are placed at studied angles between the lamp light and the observer and so calculated as to prevent the light from striking directly into his eyes, yet permitting the rays to spill over the areas around. The sizes and shapes of these louvre strips will vary with the lamp they serve as will their placement within the lamp structure.

Some are long, narrow, metal strips set in parallel with the fluorescent lamp very closely resembling venetian blinds. There are some of wider strips of metal interlocked or crisscrossed like the sectioning of an egg box. Others may be of special design, with or without perforations, extending parallel to the light rays above and/or below at the lampshade openings. There are many other schemes which work as efficient light baffles, each devised to serve its own type and style of lamp. Some of these may be so well concealed within the structure of the lamp and so well disguised as part of a structural member as to go quite unnoticed.

Another important function which the lampshade may be called upon to perform is to diffuse the emitted light partially or wholly. Semi-translucent materials used between the light source and direct vision do this job best. These may be anything from frosted or opal glass to sheer fabrics or oiled papers. There are many such which can be incorporated to serve in their direct state. Some, however, may be of a semi-transparent nature and must therefore be aided to the point of good performance. Some fabrics require double thickness in the nature of decorative net overlays or linings; others like plastics may require surface films like rubbed frostings or color sprays.

Decorative bands of opaque materials placed at judicious points along the shade like nailhead designs or thin sheet-metal laminations on mica really act as baffles but in a limited way also serve to disperse the light. Quite often, the lamp is encased by a hood or set into a globe underneath the lampshade. These devices are made of translucent glass, plastic, mica or other like material to diffuse the raw light. In a limited sort of way the light bulb itself might serve if it is frosted, if it has an opal-white globe, or if it has an enameled finish. Very often a very finely meshed plastic or wire gauze used as a clip-on hood will disperse the light rays so evenly as to create an efficient diffusing screen. If used on a pin-up or bracket lamp, it can be decorated and it can double as a shade, too.

Some lamp light requires deflection to cushion it from striking directly upon unwanted surfaces. This technique usually works hand-in-hand with the redirection of the light. If you are going to prevent light from striking off in a given direction, you must redirect it to some other point at the same time. They seem to be simultaneous acts, one being negative, the other positive. There are many methods by which this end result can be gotten, each of them excellent in its particular place.

By using reflecting surfaces, all light beams going in a given direction can be blocked and rerouted in some other given direction. As much or as little of this light may be so changed; the angle of this redirection will depend upon the shape, curvature, and the reflective power of the surface used. Much of the so-called indirect lighting is controlled in that manner. Built in reflectors, those lamps whose bowls are mirrored, may be used in less complicated situations or for temporary and/or minor adjustments. Hoods, baffles and louvres are mechanisms used to gain partial results. These devices are more efficient in deflecting light than in redirecting it. All of these schemes may be incorporated into the lampshade design or added to it as accessory appliances.

Lampshades are very influential in setting up the color notes and the group unit moods. Since most of the household lamps are white or daylight (bluish), color must be installed with the use of proper shade. The lamplight can be forced to filter through a translucent shade. This will alter the color so that the visible light is of the lampshade hue. It may, too, bounce off the inside surface of an opaque "shade". This, too, controls the kind of rays which are permitted to spill out and cover the surrounding surfaces nearby. The kind of surfaces used and their respective colors determine the color key.

Illumination may be controlled in various ways. As an overall control, the amount of illumination determined by the size of the lamplight bulb affects the entire picture—its visibility, its mood, and its decorative incident. Three-way lights, which have a double element, serve also to control the amount of illumination. First, one is heated to incandescence, then the second is turned on while the first is cut off. Finally, as a third degree of illumination, both are cut into the circuit creating a brighter light. They are generally obtainable in 50 watt, 100 watt and 150 watt combination, or 100, 200 and 300 watt arrangements. Then, too, auxiliary sockets may be screwed into place between the lamp and the fixture socket. These inserts are equipped with a swivel collar which increases the resistance in it, thereby cutting down the amount of current which can pass through the lamp itself. The light will burn brighter or duller in inverse ratio to the degree of resistance set up in this socket. Finally, there are switches installed in the lamp bases or along the extension line which rheostats the current, thus controlling the wattage efficiency of the illumination. They work on the same principle as the electric pressing iron with its multiple controls does. These methods may be used in combination with each other as well.

# Selecting the Proper Shade

Let us assume that we have already selected and made the proper lamp base for a particular need. It now becomes a problem of deciding upon the correct lamp shade for that base—correct right down to its size, shape and materials before we can proceed to make it.

We must first fully understand certain prime principles about size, shape, color and texture. We must fathom the basic relationship between lamp base and lamp shade, between lamp and the pieces in the group of which it is a part, between the lamp and the entire room decor.

First, the lamp shade must suit the lamp base as a hat suits the head and face upon which it sets. This means that it seeks the proper relationship to the base in size—not too large nor too small, and not too deep nor too shallow. Its width should set upon that of the base without seeming to cover it like an umbrella and its height should not dwarf the base and make it appear as though it has been draped with a tent. To help make such decisions a bit easier, it should first be determined whether the lamp base or the lamp shade is to be the dominant part of this combination. Like good sculpture, their relationship of size should be pleasant from every point of appearance, whether viewed from the front, the side, or from the top.

Suppose we inspect the portables—the floor and the table lamp. The height of the floor lamp and the height of the table lamp as it sets on its correct piece of furniture should be high enough to avoid looking down into it when seated or standing near it as its use demands. Neither shall the shade be so high that the person who happens to be situated next to it during its function will find himself staring into the raw pool of light from the lamp. If this situation is unavoidable, then some sort of baffle or shield should be planned which will cover this awkward escape and protect the user's sight.

The overall of the length to the height and to the width of the entire lamp should not be equal in all directions resulting in a cube-like appearance. This will prove a monotonous space arrangement and unpleasant to look at for any protracted length of time. Vary one of these dimensions and it will improve the lamp's appearance tremendously. Such variety and change should be predicated upon the decision as to which dimension should be the most effectively important one. The other measurement should then relate to that selected dominant size. Good taste is the measure of one's judgment to make selections with which most people will agree. It may be radical in its adjustment, but they must have a pleasing overtone in their relationship.

Now, the horizontal division which marks the separation of lamp and lampshade must avoid any monotonous division such as an equal one. It must, too, avoid breaking up these visual areas into such complex and/or variety of parts as to cause confusion. This marks the selection of such dividing line that the arbitration becomes a happy medium.

Further correlation between both halves of the lamp depends on their respective shapes. Such relationships are based to a great degree upon the harmonics of their basic proportions such as a circle would have to a square whose side equals the diameter, or of a rectangle and an oval with like measurement of long and short axes. Such harmony is based upon a common measurement. However, another relationship which fits this analy-

51

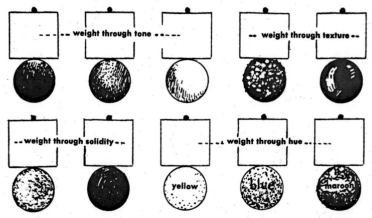

weight through tone

weight through texture

weight through solidity

weight through hue

yellow · blue · maroon

sis of relationship is based upon similarity of shape. One circle to another of different size, one square to a larger or smaller one or any such related groupings set up an agreeable situation between the parts because of their common bond of shape proportions. It is like seeing the same thing from different distances, hence the feeling of self identification with the re-identification of the parts. It's like meeting something you have met before—a sort of previous acquaintanceship with familiar elements. This rule is elastic enough to permit simultaneous recognition of two parts not quite identical, but near enough to be thought so or even to be mistaken for the same.

In the same vein of influence, there stands the identification of an element, such as a size or shape, with its multiples. Take, for example, a rectangular unit. This should be in harmony with a shape whose length is identical, but whose width is a simple and obvious multiple of it such as twice or three times its size, perhaps half or a third of it. Such a relationship may be extended beyond such low numerical relationship. It may be raised to such porportional limit as is possible for one to identify, consciously or subconsciously. Proportions like 1 to 2, 1:3, 1:4, etc. may be varied by less obvious, though easily suspected proportion as 2:3, 2:5, 3:4, 3:5 or 5:8, etc. Such proportions are not based upon absolute mathematical exactness. They are reasonably approximate and measure up to satisfy the "eye-scan" judgment of the viewer.

Another facet in the relationship of the lampshade to the lamp base based upon the "common element" idea, although less simple a thought, is the identity of such varied shapes as might be constructed within or around a given basic one. Suppose we select a square. Then the circle whose diameter is about the same size as one side of the square becomes a sister shape to it and in harmony with it. In the same manner, an equilateral or a right triangle set exactly with this square relates itself to the square and to the circle based upon this square. Such other shapes as octagons, hexagons, diagonal-pointed ovals, crosses and other not-so-easily-described shapes which are based upon this original square we had described relate to each other, to the circle previously mentioned and to any other shape so invented.

There are other factors to consider when selecting a lampshade for a lamp base. There is the element of textural harmony. This brings in the selection and matching of materials. Strongly opposing textures such as high glossy versus very dull, and smooth as against very rough, set up a conflict. While this may be desirable in small doses and set at strategic spots for accent, it is not regarded as suitable for the entire diet. Agreed that these textures should not be so alike that one cannot discern the difference between shade and base or establish their area of separation. There can be a happy medium—a relationship close enough to establish without trouble or without hesitation similarity and identity of material to material.

Such fabrics, as monk's cloth and tweeds, or materials like raffia or twine, set much better on a biscuit ceramic base than on a highly polished metal or glazed porcelain. Satins, parchments, and tole shades have greater textural agreement with these latter bases. Here we see an adjustment of textural agreement based upon the selection of materials. However, it may be approached from the point of textural finishes. For instance, a smooth fabric can assume a variety of textural qualities depending upon its final treatment and even its style of decoration. A cotton broadcloth looks different if it has been "mercerized," "coated," "loaded" or "impregnated." It changes its textural face with each type of treatment and with every change of material used in these techniques.

The happy marriage of lampshade with lamp base is very greatly influenced by color. This vitalizing factor offers the strongest "eye-appeal" in the entire situation. It draws upon the material for color supply and upon the lamplight within the lamp and about the room for additional influence. All this is aside from the fact that the juxtaposition of color spots about them—in the chairs, tables, walls, floor and ceiling—act as color controls and influences upon them.

Reds complement greens and make them seem brighter as do all opposite hues. Related colors near each other tend to dull one another. We try to seek one hue which would act as dominant above all others, yet we seek to balance the score; dark against the light hues, warm and the cool colors, the bright with the dull. All these are relative and must be judged by such standards.

Color, in all its phases, is an important factor in any combination of parts. An off-hue can strike a discordant note sufficient to cause the rejection of the entire lamp. Even after we have selected the correct hue, we must choose it in its proper tone. Too dark or too light may upset a

delicate equilibrium within the color scheme of the whole. The proper shade of the base to the shade must be selected as carefully as the proper color of nail polish or lip rouge for the occasion to be attended. This phase of color—intensity or saturation which is the brightness and dullness a color retains—is the most subtle to handle—and the most evasive. It requires a great deal of sensitive evaluation.

Aside from all these considerations, color establishes an emotional association with each viewer. This may even vary with the same person at different hours of day, month or season. This intangible quality called mood is purely subjective even though certain hues, tones or intensities may cause quite similar reactions to a broad base of people. It is this reaction to colors that causes people to prefer one color to another; it establishes favorite colors and colors to be disliked and rejected.

Once the general form of the lampshade is definitely established, it may be further related to the base through its decorative treatment. These surface embellishments take various forms. They may be a surface treatment by means of marbleized oil painting, finger paint, block prints, stencils, air brushed unit, etc. They may be additional pieces attached to the shade as with the use of tapes, ribbons and bindings, decoupage, montages and decals, beads, buttons and buckles or some such similar addenda.

The lampshade should relate to the lamp base as intimately as do a pair of hands with fingers laced in prayer. The lines of one should continue and flow into the line of the other in a completely integrated continuity. The eye should catch a major line of direction along the base and travel smoothly along the structural edges onto and along those of the shade, then should quietly and gracefully return to start a new trip along another avenue of rhythmic lines.

The greatest weight should, if it is to develop a feeling of stability, tend toward the lower areas of the lamp. However, the tendency of eye-travel should be upward toward the lighter areas of the lamp. Very often such eye-movement may direct itself along a complicated route. It may utilize many horizontal paths which may serve as interesting focal points, though they be the less important ones of the design. This is called *rhythm;* its operation is based upon related line direction.

These directed eye-movements may also be achieved by means of repetition—the repetition of a common element which staggers upward or across to terminate with the shade. These may be line, shape or color elements in any of their aspects and combinations. If, for instance, the base has as its major contour line a convex-concave edge commonly recognized as an "S" curve, then the repetition of the "Ess" curve in the lamp shade and within the decoration on it relates all parts which use such curves. An interesting historical example of this is the inclusion of "C's" and "S's" in their devices and designs by the court artists and artisans during the reign of Charles II of England.

Repetition of units of design is another form of uniting otherwise unrelated parts. This, very often, becomes the signature of an artist, of a group even of a period of production. To illustrate this further, witness the constant use of the lyre shape by Duncan Phyfe, the repeated employment of hard curves and angular lines by the group of "Modernistic" designers of the early and mid-twenties and the free use of the curule curve better known as the letter "S" by every known and unknown artistic creator during the Louis XV Period, of France. Such repetition of lines and forms need not necessarily be in entire exactness. Gradual diminishment of en-

54

largement constitutes a particular kind of such repetition called progression. Even colors ranging from dark to light, bright to dull, warm to cool and vice versa, fall under this type of rhythmic relationship. These, the lamp shade and the lamp base, can be made to form a family bond through the use of textural ties. A coarse kind of ceramic lamp base invites the use of a knubby, loose-woven cloth; a highly polished wooden base should receive a shade covered with semi-matte cloth like a cotton or linen shantung. Likewise, a highly polished metal or porcelain base should be accompanied by a fine silk, taffeta, moire of satiny texture to match.

All this should be handled with a fine sense of balance—balance of many kinds. First, the sense of stability of the entire lamp must be established. The shade should not appear to be too heavy, too large or too wide so that an overpowering inverted feeling is created. Conversely, there shouldn't be established a feeling of "bareheadedness" when the bottom section, the lamp base, overpowers the combination. The distribution of attraction throughout the lamp ensemble by means of line, form, color and texture should be as sensitively balanced as a graceful dancer during an intricate or delicate dance step.

In determining the form of the lamp shade, we must look at it from several positions and its form must appear as pleasant from each individually and as a group. The more popular positions to look at the lamp are 1) the side view, either left or right or both and, 2) the top view. The proportions of the side or vertical view are naturally dependent upon those of the lamp base and vice versa. The top shape of the shade should, too, be harmonious with that of the lamp base. Keeping this in mind, one may borrow lines and forms from one to be used with the other part as harmonic and rhythmic repeats.

Basic lamp shade forms as seen from the top fall into a group of simple geometric shapes. With slight variation, these are consistent throughout. It holds true for the top edge of the shade as well as the bottom.

The general classifications of top view shapes of lamp shades fall into these groups:
1. Round—those based upon the circle.
2. Oval—those whose contours are elongated circles regardless of the degree or its ratio between the long and short axis.
3. Flatted Oval—is really circular at each end and straight lined between these ends. The elongation has no other relationship to the circular ends than the short and long sides of a rectangle have to each other.
4. Square—has four equal sides and creates panels along the front and end view surfaces.
5. Triangular—generally based upon the equilateral triangle. This goes well with the square or the circle.
6. Rectangular—an adaptation of the square when only greater width is needed for the area of illumination.
7. Polygonic—in which a shape of any given number of straight sides greater than four is used to frame vertical panels along the side of the frame.

While the top and bottom rims of the frame may be alike in shape, they need not necessarily be so. One edge may be similar though smaller, or be dissimilar but harmonious, as would a square bottom line up with an octagon of the same altitude.

The vertical or side view of the frame fits another grouping of shapes.

These views are dependent upon the top and bottom lampshade shape to a great extent. For example, a straight-sided shape may be considered as a "drum design" if the top and bottom are circles; a cube, if they are squares, and a plinth or column form if the extremities are of polygonic, oval, or any other odd or combined shapes.

These are the major side view groups and they will vary when applied to differently shaped top or bottom views:

1. SQUARE—called a cube or box shade if combined with a square or rectangular base and a drum shade if used with a round or oval shape. Top and bottom rims must be of the same size to keep the sides straight.

2. CONCAVE—is a sort of inward or "knock-kneed" bend along the sides. This, too, can be combined with a variety of top view shapes; round, oval, square, rectangular, etc. It requires that the top rim be smaller than the larger as a rule.

3. CONVEX—whose extreme example is a domed shade. Variations of this range from the completely closed dome to one allowing an open ring on top about the size of the bottom ring like the inverted teacup shape.

4. TRIANGULAR shade is either a cone or a pyramid. These may close to a point on top as some of the modern shades are, or truncated to allow an opening.

5. TRAPEZOIDAL shade is a variation of the square using a smaller top frame than a bottom one.

6. NOVELTY forms are developed by combining two or more of these basic vertical shapes and setting them upon assorted rims.

A vari-paneled shade can be developed by using a square base hitched to an octagonal top rim and running vertical wire from lower corners to relative upper corners. Setting it on a circular base should create an interestingly new shade form.

A wave-curved bell shade will result when a square base rim is fastened to a square top with multiple curved, waved wires from upper to corresponding lower corners. Further variation of this theme can be gotten if the square shaped rims become triangular, rectangular, or round.

The "S"-shaped bell shade is another achievement of combining basic lines. This curule curved lampshade may be built upon a square, triangular, rectangular or polygonic base rim. It precludes the use of a like but smaller top rim.

Other novelty shades can grow out of the combination of several shallow forms. The "pagoda" shape may be the combination of a drum and truncated concaved pyramid. It may be a series of such pyramids, one set upon the other so that the top rim of one serves as the base rim of the one above. A truncated pyramid set upon and topped by straight-sided collars is an added change. These can go on ad infinitum or as long as the permutations and combinations hold out a helping hand to the designer's imagination. Greater variation can be heaped upon this load by changing the proportion of the parts within each possible combination of top and vertical shapes.

When we talk of decoration and trim, we must determine the edges along which we intend to set them. Some of the more obvious points are along the top and bottom rims of the lampshade. Generally, these are straight edges. They can, however, be bent or cut to other shapes and by this method affect an accent along those lines. In addition to or instead of this, accents may be created by the addition of trim strips like fringes, tassels, ribbons, beads, etc.

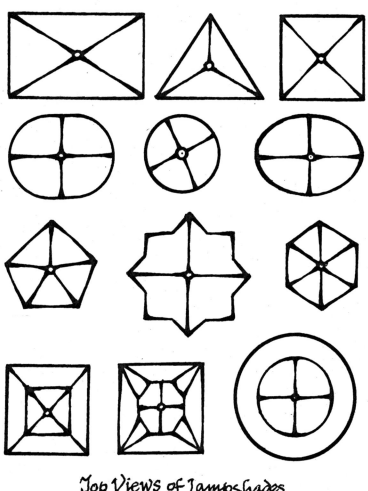

Top Views of Lampshades

Lampshade Shapes

One rhythmic scheme is to repeat the form of the top or bottom rim in shorter units in a continuous run around these edges in the vertical view. Should the top view show a circle, the bottom rim wire might be bent into a circular looped scalloped edge or an alternate half circle as a waved edge. The square suggests a squared fret, the rectangle a deep or shallow fret repeat. These units grow out of the form and contour of the whole.

These edge shapes may be subdivided into a few basic groups such as 1) the straight edge; 2) the convex; 3) the concave; 4) the serpentine; 5) the scalloped; 6) the fluted; 7) the waved; 8) the serrated; 9) the fretted and 10) the notched.

In addition to this, trimmings may be used to assist any of these edge accents or to create one of its own. We are acquainted with the tasseled trim, the fringed edge, the ruffled edge, the festooned, the braided, the shirred, the button, the beaded or the nailhead trim.

When selecting the lampshade for its base, it should be remembered that this combination must achieve certain visual values through the basic principles of design: dominance, rhythm, and balance.

We have just seen the steps utilized in gaining a rhythmic relationship between the two by means of repetition of lines, forms, tones, colors, textures, and materials and their close harmonics.

We can establish a sense of dominance within the shade or the lamp base depending upon which suits the design best. This can be best achieved by means of contrasts. This seems quite far afield from the methods used in gaining rhythm. These contrasts may appear as opposition of line directions. The shade may be a horizontal drum on a vertical square plinth or a base made up of a bundle of vertical bamboo tubes. To further accent this contrast, the shade may be wrapped horizontally with hemp twine.

Another means of achieving dominance is through the contrast of form. A square plinth of a shade set upon a spheroidal base points up one in contrast to the other. Further selection for emphasis may be gotten by adding the design units upon the lampshade or the base, whichever has been determined the most important of the two by means of decoration. This decoration may be on the shade material as in the nature of print, applique or decoupage or additional trimming materials like decorative tape, fringed borders or festooned ribbon.

The most effective factor in creating the accent upon shade or lamp base is through the application of color in any or all of its aspects. Use of contrasting hues can point up the importance of one part of the lamp. Suppose the lamp is of a soft, dull tone set upon and within similar hues; by making the shade of a totally different hue such as green among browns or orange among blues, contrast is established.

Another facet of color contrast in addition to hue is that of tone. A light shade over a dark base set among dark tones of the group sets off the lampshade as outstanding. Conversely, a dark shade set upon a lighter surrounding, regardless of the combination of the hues, will also stand out. In the same vein, a bright color will stand out in sharp contrast against a larger mass of dull colors. Here, the lampshade has the added advantage of the light bulb in its favor. If it is a translucent shade, the illumination behind it adds greater intensity to the color of the lampshade. Should it be of opaque material, the light which emanated from behind it affects a nimbus—a glow which emphasizes the shade against its background and surroundings.

Further emphasis may be accomplished by accenting the weight of one as opposed to the other part. If the particular shade calls for an airiness;

a pierced, perforated or porous textured material can supply this quality to the shade. If it is intended to produce the opposite effect, reverse the process by using a solid, coarse-textured material for the lampshade.

These are all general suggestions to follow when selecting a lampshade to suit a lamp base. The specific suggestions are intended to answer particular points of relationship as the designer meets them during the process of determining proper factors and their relative replies to them. To use them with intelligence, with sound judgment and with good taste is to insure worthwhile and good-looking results in lamp unity.

Besides all of these "rules" for "good taste", it must be remembered that the lamp—base and shade—is basically an instrument which must function well within its surroundings and toward its goal. It must supply the correct amount of light for good visibility and serve its job well. It should offer the right type of illumination—direct, indirect, or both—and the correct color and tone to accompany this illumination, whether in high, middle or low key so that the mood and temper is available to match the "stage setting" of the room.

At times the designer may simply repeat in the shade the curves or lines of the base, giving them a broader sweep in harmony with the larger area. Subtleties of curve may be so accented that attention is called to them.

In the treatment of the necessarily strong horizontal line at the bottom of the shade, there may be the feeling that it terminates too abruptly before arriving at the curves of the shape or base.

The architectural severity of the base, be it wood, metal, ceramics, etc., demands that the shade be treated more or less architecturally. This line may be softened or made less conspicuous by curving the skeletal wires or treating the line with additional material which will tie it more firmly in with the lines, forms and color of the entire lamp design.

Texture is a subtle element. It may be suggested by color, surface gloss, by feeling of weight, by "richness" of materials, by the density and visual strength of the material and by the results of the techniques and methods used to make and decorate the lampshade. Obviously, there is a cross-influence of all these factors with the word "texture" attempting to describe this elusive feeling. Nevertheless, it is there and must be considered in its proper importance. It cannot be wished aside.

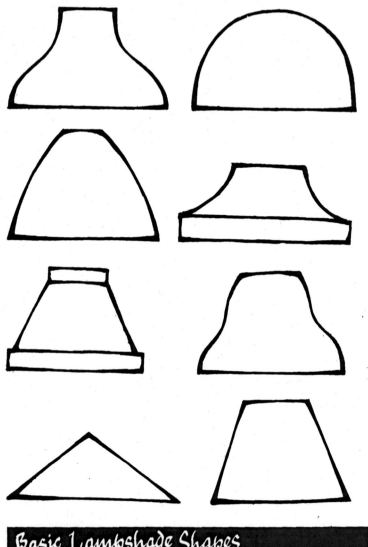

**Basic Lampshade Shapes**

**Lampshade Edges**

60

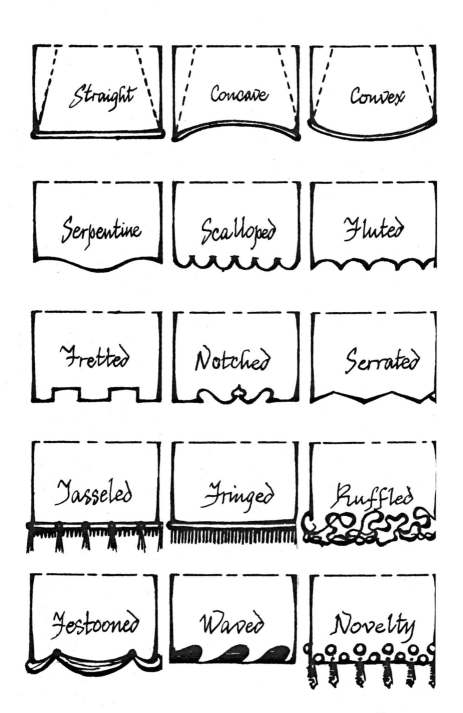

Straight

Concave

Convex

Serpentine

Scalloped

Fluted

Fretted

Notched

Serrated

Tasseled

Fringed

Ruffled

Festooned

Waved

Novelty

61

# Materials of the Lampshade

There are actually no specific guides nor limitations to the kinds of materials of which lampshades can be made. Because this is true, some interesting and unusual combinations are achieved. The selection becomes one of personal taste and physical adaptation to its function. They run the gamut of metals to paper, fibers to fur—individually and in combination.

Basically, these materials fall into three classes: the *transparent* such as glass and plastics might be, *translucent* as exemplified by fabrics, certain papers and *opaque* as are metals and wood. Since the lampshades are set high on the lamp structure and is usually the largest part of it, it must be made of such material that will keep its weight at a minimum. This is intended to maintain the balance of weight at a low level and create greater stability. Hence, it is evident that the larger the shade, the lighter its material must be. The larger the shade, the wider the base or the lower a center of gravity must be maintained.

It may be desirable to list all those materials which fall within each group. But this is not as simple as it sounds since some of these may be transparent, translucent and/or opaque, depending upon some of its component parts, its method of fabrication and/or decoration. Glass is an excellent example of this. Clear window pane is transparent, however, if frosted, opal, tinted or variegated on one side, it becomes translucent. Finally, if pigment has been added in its original manufacture, it may be as opaque as the marble or onyx. Similar illustrations can be made with plastic materials, fabrics, skins and papers.

We must assume that these materials we intend to describe merely serve as the covering over of some type of frame. Other methods of constructing the lampshade will be discussed in section so labeled. Furthermore, these materials are prepared and worked on in various ways. These, too, we shall investigate.

Since most frames for the lamp base are constructed out metal, it would be the logical material with which to start. *Metal* foil of heavier gauge is cut to fit the shade shape. This is rolled gently over the top and bottom rims and fastened to it. Some metal cements like Pliobond are available and on the market. These can be used to hold the joint firmly. Where copper-base metals like bronze, brass, copper, even sheet iron and tin are used, it may be soft soldered along strategic spots and seams. Short metal "U" clips make convenient clamps to be pressed over the rounded edge. Designs may be pressed or scored into the metal with tools that resemble blunted ice picks and nut picks.

Punched decoration is another form of handling and a cross-variation of the two is gotten by incising part of the picture contours and raising other parts slightly from its background. This will permit the lamp light to filter through and accent the silhouete images on the shade. All these are impressed upon the sheet metal before it is fastened to the frame.

Many novelty variations of sheet metal decoration have been explored by lampshade makers. Some of the more obvious are: 1) using vertical slots cut either vertically or horizontally across the surface, then lacing ribbons of contrasting metal, plastic film, fabric, leather, wood veneers, etc. to create a woven, all-over pattern; 2) to punch a series of pre-planned holes through which plastic, leather or cloth lace is stitched to create a continuous line picture or one resembling the old time sampler; 3) to use nailheads or silhouette cut-outs added to the surface of the shade; 4) to paint, stencil, spray, paste decals or flock a design at focal points of the lampshade, and many variations and combinations too numerous to permit classification. We should not overlook the fact that metal thread and metallic cloth is available which can be used like any other fabric.

*Wooden* shades are hardly used except in functional modern design. The nature of the material lends itself to few and limited forms. Solid and heavy wood is quite the rare

## ADHESIVES
**Numbers indicate the quantity of each material used**

| | |
|---|---|
| Wood glue: | 1 gelatin, 2 water and heat. Add 1 glacial acetic acid. |
| Marine glue: | 12 Para'caoutchouc in 12 benzol. Add 20 powdered shellac. Heat mixture carefully. |
| Waterproof glue: | 55 gelatin glue and water. Add potassium bichromate and alum. |
| Paper paste: | Flour and water and sugar (glucose). |
| Paper paste: | Gum arabic, white sugar and water. |
| Paper paste: | Paste of flour and alum or zinc chloride solution in water. |
| Paper paste: | 10 starch, 5 sugar, ½ zinc chloride mixed in water. |
| Celluloid cement: | 2 shellac, 3 spirits of camphor, 4 strong alcohol. Heat. |
| Cutler's cement: | 4 rosin, 1 beeswax, and 1 plaster of Paris. |
| Stone cement: | 4 gypsum, 1 finely powdered gum arabic. Add borax. |
| Iron cement: | 30 plaster of Paris, 10 iron filings, ½ salamoniac and vinegar. |
| Glass cement: | 2 litharge, 1 white lead add to 3 boiled linseed oil and 1 copal varnish. |
| Glass cement: | 150-96% acetic acid, 100 gelatin (heat). Add 5 ammonium bichromate. (Keep from light.) |
| Glass cement: | Canada balsam. |
| Waterglass cement: | Sodium or potassium silicate and casein paste. |
| Paper cement: | 5 chloral hydrate, 8 gelatin white, 2 gum arabic in 30 boiling water. |
| Rubber cement: | Pure gum rubber in white gasoline or naphtha. Shake daily. |
| Rubber cement: | 100 India rubber (finely chopped), 15 rosin, 10 shellac, add carbon disulphide to dissolve. |
| Acid proof cement: | 2 sodium silicate, 1 sand, 1 asbestos. Mix. |
| Strong cement: | 12½ boiled linseed oil and 12½ castor oil and casein. Boil, add aqueou alum. Pour off milky fluid. Add 120 rock candy syrup and 6 dextrin to residue. |
| Universal cement: | 100 gum arabic, 75 starch, 21 white sugar, 4 camphor, dissolve individually, mix and boil until paste. |
| Miscellaneous: | Litharge and glycerine (glass, stone, etc.), 10 starch, 5 sugar, ½ zinc chloride mixed in water. |

medium for it is functionally far too heavy except in unusually large lamps. The use of one-sixteenth inch or thinner plywood is reserved for flat surfaces linked to form hollow geometric forms. They may be lashed together with fancy cords, leather or plastic laces or woven cloth tapes. They may be joined in the traditional manner with glue, angle irons and rivets, grooved showcase moldings or plastic corner moldings. Thin strips of wood of varied widths ranging from one-half to about three inches may be woven basket-fashion to fit around a lampshade frame. Fine grains, carefully matched and finished should result in some very interesting textural patterns. For greater variety, these strips may be stained or dyed to add colorful glamour and accent.

In the same tradition, the frame may be covered with lengths of split bamboo, pointed or not, neatly lashed together near the top and bottom edges. Fine reed or braided raffia might be used. Cord and laces make excellent substitutes as tie-strings. For that matter, reed woven in basket-like manner and to round, oval or any other shape should be equally good. The edges might be loop-finished over the top or bottom edges as the bread-baskets usually are. An alternate way of concluding this reed shade is to trim it along the edges with narrow, decorative flat face-molding. This is, of course, simple to apply to a flat-sided lampshade, but somewhat less acceptable to curved surfaces.

We must not preclude the use of cork as a medium. This

## WOODS

| NAME | CHARACTERISTICS | NAME | CHARACTERISTICS |
|---|---|---|---|
| Alder | Red-brown. Fine even grain. Hard. | Oak | Heavy, tough and strong. |
| Applewood | Hard. | Pine | Light to heavy—soft to hard. |
| Ash | White or red. Strong and stiff. | Poplar | Light, soft, durable, fine grain. |
| Basswood | White, even grain. Light, soft, weak. | Redwood | Very soft and light. Straight grain and durable. |
| Beech | Heavy. Hard and strong. | Spruce | Light, soft, stiff and strong. |
| Birch | Red, yellow, white. Heavy, tough hard and strong. | | Even grain. |
| Butternut | Like black walnut—heavy. | Sycamore | Tough, strong, hard to split. |
| Cedar | Light and soft. Even grain. Resists decay. | Tamarack | Very heavy, strong, tough and durable. |
| Cherry | Dense and strong. Wears well. | Tupelo | Medium weight, close grain, hard to split. |
| Chestnut | Light and soft. Durable. | Black Walnut | Hard, heavy, rich color, close grain. |
| Cottonwood | Light and soft. Even grain. Resists wear. | Willow | Very light and soft—tough. |
| Cypress | Strong, heavy, durable. | Rosewood | Beautiful grain, hard, dark color, tough. |
| Elm | Light, tough and fibrous. | Mahogany | White to dark red. Close grain, beautiful, hard, tough. |
| Fir | Light, soft, even grain, not too strong | Satinwood | Gray, hard, strong, striated grain. |
| Gum | Black, red, stiff, hard, tough and strong. | Teak | Straw colored, tough, strong, hard, heavy. |
| Hemlock | Light, stiff, strong and tough. | Zebrawood | Alternate striping of 2-tone gray, hard, tough. |
| Hickory | Heavy, strong, tough and shockproof. | Tulipwood | Striated red and cream colored, medium weight. |
| Holly | Close grain and tough. | | |
| Magnolia | Compact, light, soft, satin luster. White to light brown. | Amaranth | Purpleheart. Very hard, tough, close grain. |
| Maple | Medium weight. Strong and hard. | Ebony | Dark to black. Tough, strong, heavy. |
| Hairwood | Gray-striated, strong, hard, close grain, heavy. | | |
| Lignum Vita | Very heavy, hard and strong. | | |

| PAPER | | | | |
|---|---|---|---|---|
| **KINDS** | **FORMING TECHNIQUES** | **METHODS OF DECORATION** | | **FINISHING** |
| Tissue | Glueing | Dyeing | Hectograph | Plastic spray |
| Newsprint | Gummed | Staining | Multigraph | Impregnation |
| Kraft | Stapled | Batik | Spraying | Shellac |
| Plyboard | Stitched | Painting | Spattering | Varnish |
| Pressedwood | | Marbleizing | Decoupage | Oil paint |
| Maché | | Stenciling | Montage | Lacquer |
| Pulp | | Block Printing | Overlaying | |
| | | | Underlaying | |

material comes in flat sheets of almost any thickness and in varying closeness of texture. Use it as you might any hard solid covering material like paper, parchment, etc. It is very flexible and can be bent to conform to almost any shape without cracking, depending upon the thickness of the cork. Its surface offers practically all the leeway of decoration as does paper with few exceptions. It may also be treated as wood and finished in a like manner.

Wood veneers have been glued on to linen-back and used as a heavy wallpaper. Why not then as lampshade covering? This material is excellent for flat paneling. It can also be stretched around a curved surface, but it must be bent with the grain, else it will crack. It is procurable in about twenty or more different kinds of wood offering a wide variety of grain and texture and a full latitude of their respective colors. Every treatment and finish one can apply to wood can, of course, be used on this material. Some of the cardboard techniques are likely here such as decoupage, stencils, etc.

*Paper* offers a very wide field of choice for lampshade material. First, there are the vast varieties of kinds like flex-ply, crepe, newsprint, etc., multiplied by their textural treatment and decoration. Marbleizing, flocking, block printing, linen textured, metalized, leather pressed, etc., are just some of these. Combine these with their limitless color possibilities and you have a world from which to choose.

In addition to the kinds of paper available, there are the many methods of working with them. Aside from using them in flat sheet form, some papers may be embossed, tooled to look like leather, cut into strips and woven bas-

---

**CONDITIONS FOR APPLYING**
*Pastes, Glues and Cements*

1. Heat parts to make them plastic. Hold until cool and firmly fixed.
2. Heat adjourning surfaces.
3. Applying a solvent. Hold together until hard, again.
4. Apply adhesive, setting affected by chemical action.
5. Apply adhesive with a volatile solvent. Allow it to evaporate.
6. Apply adhesive, setting affected by hydration of body parts.
7. Apply adhesive, setting affected by oxidation.
8. Apply heated adhesive, setting affected by cooling action.

| CERAMICS | | | |
| --- | --- | --- | --- |
| PRODUCED BY | DECORATION | MATERIALS | PROPERTIES |
| Casting<br>Jiggering<br>Throwing<br>Pressing | Biscuit firing<br>Gloat firing<br>Hand painting<br>Copperplate<br>Decalcomania<br>Gold applique<br>(stamped or painted) | Kaolin or<br>China clay<br><br>Ball or blue<br>clay<br><br>Flint<br><br>Bone ash<br><br>Feldspar<br><br>China stone | Very strong, keeps its form, purest and whitest.<br>Very strong, white and absorbent, can be mixed with Kaolin.<br>Stands high temperatures. Keeps its shape well.<br>Strong, white and keeps shape well.<br>Melts quickly and serves to unite other materials.<br>Acts as flux. Gives translucency. |

ket-fashion and twisted into string to be wound, wrapped, knotted and knitted to resemble fibers and fabrics. They may even be impregnated or coated to feel and look like metal, wood and plastic materials.

Special treatment of paper adds many more selections for lampshade coverings. Old prints or replicas of the popular Currier and Ives or the Audubons are interesting when cemented on to some translucent shade which permits the lamp behind it to cause it to glow with fluorescent brightness. Old maps attached to "parchment" paper which has been antiqued with "coffee or tea stains" to show paper aging or the "crinkle-wrinkle" and the "wash-out" water color dip are two other tricky effects. The method of wiping oil into the paper is an old stunt, but still effectively used as a substitute for vellum.

*Plastics* is the generic term for all synthetic resin materials. They are all thermoplast and thermoset materials regardless of what trade names they are called. When these resins are in the liquid stage, they are classified as "A-Stage Resins." They will remain in that state indefinitely until the polymerizing or curing process starts whether aided by internal or external heat. After it reaches the jelly state, it remains as a "B-Stage Resin." By allowing the curing process to reach its completion and the plastic material solid, it then becomes the "C-Stage Resin." Each of these stages has its particular use.

Lampshade frames can be covered with a plastic film. The cross-ribbing of the frame structure plus the reinforce-

| GLASS | |
| --- | --- |
| COLOR | MATERIAL ADDED |
| Amber | Coke, coal, or charcoal and sulphur |
| Black | Manganese, cobalt, or iron and carbon |
| Blue | Cobalt oxide |
| Green | Iron oxide and chromium oxide |
| Iridescent | Silver and bismuth |
| Red | Copper oxide, gold chloride and selenium |
| White | Tin or fluorspar |
| Yellow | Uranium oxide |
| Violet | Manganese oxide |

ment of large open areas must be properly assembled before it is dipped into the liquid plastic solution. This liquid resin may be stained with dyes to create a range of translucent colors. If pigment is stirred into the "A-Stage," it causes the resulting plastic to become opaque as well as colored. Fluorescent or pearlescent materials added will create special effects as will metallic filings, fiber threads, colored sands and spangle materials.

Sheet plastics are made in flexible or rigid sheets in gauges ranging from paper thinness to thickness of approximately two inches. Here, too, they are made to resemble a vast latitude of material other than the smooth plastic surface. Imitations of practically every type of leather, mother of pearl, mottlings, striations, moires, variegations of spots, lace and cloth—plain and prints. Textural embossments are not limited either. Pebble, leather and wood grains, all kinds of textile weaves, knitted and crocheted stitches, laces, braid and flexible molding strips are some of the plastic aids for the lampshade craftsman.

Obviously, the very thick, stiff and/or heavy plastics have limited calls as lampshade materials. We must recognize that it is the thinner stock and the flexible variety which most often finds favor in that direction. The rigid material is more applicable to the flat-sided geometric forms used in lampshade design.

There are many ways of assembling plastic materials. Like leather or stiff paper, holes may be punched along the edges and lashed to the frame using any of the many kinds of leather-lace stitching. Metal, leather or plastic clips of assorted lengths will do when riveted into place. Likewise with thin stock angle irons and joining plates. Plastic adhesives are not to be overlooked. In some cases "wet-welds" are gotten easily where a plastic solvent is feasible. Adhesive bonding agents are the next most likely method. Here it becomes necessary to use the correct cement for the material used. It would be much more effective if the frame ribs were first coated with some plastic adherent to permit the cement to stick to that as well.

Surface decoration that can be used on plastics challenges the limits of these pages. There are so many approaches and so many variations within each. Since plastics has so many properties resembling those of metal, it is en-

| GLASS | | | | |
|---|---|---|---|---|
| FORMING METHODS | JOINING TECHNIQUES | POLISHING MATERIALS | METHODS OF DECORATING | DRILLING METHODS |
| Scratch-cutting | Water glass | Emery lap | Gray carving | Triangular file |
| Blowing | Litharge | Grindstone | Etching | Diamond bit |
| Casting | Corner plates | Rouge-rub | Sand blasting | Metal tube |
| Heat-bending | Angle irons | | Cut-glass | Clay wall and |
| | Channel- | | faceting | sludge |
| | moulding | | Mirror-plating | Kerosene and |
| | | | Outside-plating | emery |
| | | | Enameling | |

tirely possible to transfer some of the decorative operation from that material. It may be engraved, scribed and scored, pierced, carved internally and in low relief, painted on, stencilled, air brushed, lacquered, etc. It can be worked with wood techniques such as being dyed, decal pasted, branded, veneered or use paper decorative or glass treated surfaces like frosting, crackling, etc.

Speaking of *glass* as a lampshade medium makes one think a bit. We know that glass may be made of many formulas, each designed to add or subtract some property to fill a particular need. Of course, these lampshades which might use glass, might do so in combination with other materials. There are some lamp requirements where it might have exclusive domain, take for instance the torchiere group. Many glass bowls are in demand for this. Glass may be formed by *casting*. These are generally designed for use for a standard, widely-used design, or else made specifically for some manufacturer.

However, *spun glass* is woven into a textile which may be handled much the same as cloth might be. The only realization of the difference is when adhesives are needed or joints are to be made. Glass need not be used simply as clear transparent material. It comes in all opaque and translucent hues of uniform, mottled, mirrored, striated, patterned, variated and novelty effect. These may be used as strip louvres and baffles, cut to specific contours as inserts in opaque lampshades, or heat bent to suit particular design forms as galleries, panels or overlay patterns. Any intelligent survey of glass decoration should expose many, many more means of decorative surface treatment of glass; leaded, painted, gray carved, faceted, etc.

The field of *fabrics* is the backbone of the lampshade industry since the material is available in such abundance and in such great variety—sufficient to meet every style of decoration and every particular individual needs.

## TEXTILES

| MATERIALS | | WEAVES | | DECORATIONS | FINISHING |
|---|---|---|---|---|---|
| Cotton | Animal fibers: | Plain: | Knitted: | Bleaching | Sizing |
| Linen | Mohair | Basket | Jersey | Dyeing: | Mercerizing |
| Wool | Camel's hair | Rib | Pure | Stock | Lisle |
| Silk | Alpaca | Twill | Rib | Yarn | Napping |
| Man-made: | Vicuna | Satin | Tricot | Piece | Calendering |
| Rayon | Llama hair | Figure: | Milanese | Cross | Anti-crease |
| Nylon | Cashmere | Jacquard | Lace: | Printing: | Sanforizing |
| Saran | Horsehair | Pile: | Bobin | Block | Water-repellent |
| Vinylite | Artificial fibers: | Velvet | Crochet | Direct | |
| Other plastics | Metallic wire | Carpet | Darned | Warp | |
| Vegetable fibers: | Metallic tinsel | Corduroy | Needlepoint | Discharge | |
| Ramie | Paper | Terrycloth | Machine: | Resist | |
| Jute | Lastex | Gauze or Leno | Shadow | Batik | |
| Coir | Spun glass | Loppet | Princess | Stencil | |
| Kapok | Slag wool | | Oriental | Weaving: | |
| Hemp | | | | Hard and | |
| Straw | | | | Soft twist | |
| | | | | Colored yarn | |
| | | | | Moire | |

For every property exhibited by any of the other lampshade materials, there is some fabric which can match it. There are those sheer textiles which are fairly transparent, those materials which are as opaque as the heaviest of metal or wood. Then we find in this vast conglomerate collection pile fabrics to resemble furs, glazed and coated materials which go well with ceramics and pottery, coarse weaves to mate with stone or wood of rougher hew and novelty textiles to answer any and all calls made of it. Most interesting is the limitless variety offered by the combinations of weaves, yarn, color and finish which are produced by both hand and machine manufacture.

The group classified as *"skins"* includes such materials as the different furs, the many kinds of leather in all their variations of treatment and finishes. Many modern lampshades have used the flat furs for its decorative markings, its texture and probable color. Parchment and vellum belong to this division of skins. The former is prepared from the hide of the sheep, the latter is goatskin. Between these two extremes lies the whole range of prepared hides—the *leathers.*

These come in different thicknesses depending upon the kind of animal from which it is taken, the animal's age and how it has been prepared; namely if it has been skived, softened and stamp textured.

Leathers are rarely used as a lampshade covering especially since it must be kept pliable and in condition and since it can be substituted by the less expensive coated fabrics which looks so much like the original that one would have to examine it closely to really detect the difference.

All sorts of *novelty* materials have been utilized for lampshade purposes, some transient, some fashionable for a short stay, some remaining longer to become a staple item

## LEATHER

| KINDS | PROCESSES | DECORATIONS | FINISHES |
|---|---|---|---|
| Rawhide | Suede | Embroideries: | Wax |
| Cowhide and | Patent leather | Crochet | Tanned |
| calfskin | Sole leather | Rows | Patent |
| Goat and kidskins | Belt leather | Paris point | Plastic spray |
| Sheep and lambskins | Harness and saddle | Spear point | Oiled |
| Horsehide and | leather | Tambour | Saddle soap |
| coltskin | Dressed leather | Piqué | |
| Kangaroo skin | Degrained | Dyeing | |
| Elk, deer and | Glacé | Painting | |
| antelope hide | Tanning | Tooling: | |
| Pigskin | Buffing | Gilt and | |
| Buffalo hide | Matting or satin | Blind | |
| Ostrich skin | Graining or | Stamping | |
| Walrus hide and | embossed | Punching or | |
| sealskin | Snuffed or | piercing | |
| Sharkskin | corrected | Appliqué | |
| Alligator skin | Skiving | Lacing | |
| Snakeskin and | Split grain | Stitching | |
| lizard skin | Top grain | Braiding and | |
| Parchment and | | Weaving | |
| vellum | | Nail-heads | |

for perhaps a seasonal session or a more protracted period of time. One might see a basket-like shade, woven of straw like some lady's hat except more along the lines and general form of a lampshade, set into a porch or playroom decoration. It is not unlikely that this fiber shade will be altogether in place, might even be attractive in its particular setting. Such weavings have been cleverly arranged in a multitude of interesting latticed weaves and in many attractive combinations of color.

Many interesting lampshades have been on display in the local department stores, shapes for use in children's rooms which were made of string, cord or raffia. Witness some of the early Russell Wright lamp designs and note the very clever use he made of cord-wrapping sans color. String and cord of different materials—cotton, hemp, linen, paper— create individual textures and tone quality when dyed. Raffia falls in the same class of fiber fabrication that the others do. By and large this group can indulge in laced and interlaced designs, the wrapping, winding and weaving techniques of assembling, knotting, knitting and crocheting construction, and the many other methods which may cross this craft's horizon.

However, this group is not entirely limited to the use of fibers alone. Minerals like mica and isinglas have found favor before in many interesting lampshade forms. These may be used alone or in combination with plastics, metal, leather, etc. Their judicious use in design will determine to a great extent whether they fit or not. The fault will not lie with the material per se, but with the manner and taste it is utilized.

Lampshades made of tape, trimming, ruffles and braid have their particular places in the decorative scheme. These items smack of femininity, extending to the military and formal touch at the other extreme. Their association with a theme will naturally depend upon the kind and style of the material used. Lace ruffles would be more closely associated with the older females than starched or dotted Swiss and pale-colored cords do not fill the same bill of requirements that velvet or braided metallic ones would. The picture of novel and unusual materials used for lampshades is certainly not a limited one nor is it circumscribed by any precedence other than good taste. With the constant development of new materials, the field is wide open and exposes an ever-changing horizon as seen by the extending use of fluorescent fabrics.

# Lampshade Making Methods

There are not many basically different ways of making a lampshade, but within each form innumerable variations are invented. This is what gives the fresh perspective to lamp design and creates a chain of ever-changing styles.

Let us examine these basic approaches. But for the sake of simplicity we shall only consider those which meet the needs of the floor lamp and its smaller counterparts, the table lamp and the pin-up variety. This implies no logical development, sequence, or relationship between them.

First there is the panelled type with no specific frame construction. As the parts are assembled, the lampshade becomes a unit, each section being an integral part of it. A specific illustration of this is the use of four, five or six rectangular panels cut out of sheet mica, plastics or possibly thin cardboard. These are joined side to side by lace, cement or gummed binding tape to form a plinth. Each section may be used with raw, impregnated, bound, taped or reinforced panel-edges, whichever suits the needs or convenience. A top panel is then secured to the top of this open box. This panel should have a hole drilled at its exact center through which the lamp-harp's screw is fastened to fit over the lamp.

Another one of this type of shade is the one made by folding a sheet of parchment or two-ply cardboard accordion-fashion. Punch a series of aligned holes just below the top edge and thread a tasseled cord through them. In the threading, wind or lash this cord around an oval or circular wire ring having soldered cross-wires, lashed at its intersection to a wide washer. The lower end of this shade is held in fixed position by a similarly threaded cord or cement. A variation of this theme is made by cutting a plywood panel to serve as a large wooden washer to be fastened to the harp. Fine, flexible wire screen or plastic mesh is gathered closely and fastened around the edge of this disc. The joint is covered with flat plastic molding or narrow upholsterer's tape to disguise it. The lower edge which may be tape-bound, folded under or left raw should drape itself in gracefully set folds. Many variations are possible in this manner of construction.

A second type of lampshade fabrication is the covered *skeletal frame*. In this a bare frame much like that of the umbrella and made of soldered, welded, wound or clipped wires, bars or tubes. A minimum number of ribs are cross-braced to support the lampshade "skin." In a regular geometric form only two horizontal ribs are required. If the vertical ribs are complex lines, an added horizontal should be added at those points of sharp change. The joints must be polished smooth and the wires painted or lacquered for added protection. Following this, the lampshade is covered and trimmed.

Baling wire of about 11 gauge suits most needs. Since these wires are nearly always covered with binding tape of some kind, it serves little purpose to select fancy shaped or twisted wires for this purpose.

Flat metal bars of required width and thickness may be substituted for these round wires. These are generally reserved for the points of greatest strain, the top and bottom rims. On occasion, rectangular tubing of like measurements may be used if available and feasible. In order to make sharp, squared-off bends, "Vee" notches should be cut at the inside point of the bend. Soldered reinforcement of these bends help, but may not be necessary if notched correctly. For a 90 degree bend, the notch should be cut two-thirds of the thickness if solid, and right through to the front face if it is of tubing. Avoid round tubing because it is difficult to bend unless by a practiced craftsman.

Sometimes these ribs are part of the whole shade construction. Tape a modern design of a table lamp where a flexible-cable gooseneck pipe rises from a wood or stone base and supports a parabolic opaque, perhaps metal, reflector. Three or four ribs joined to a collar band below the reflector extend upward in a flare holding up an "L" shaped rim. A round Fresnel lens fits snugly down by a spring ring wire set over it and clamping the lens in place. Here the ribs are not disguised and might be of square, octagonal wires held straight or spiral twisted shape. Even double wire twisting may be used for adding effect. They are functionally frank and starkly decorative.

A third type is the *lattice-laced*. This may be finished in many ways. It may be used as a base frame through whose holes assorted lace, ribbon, wool yarns, etc. can be threaded to create interesting and colorful patterns against the latticed background. In such cases the frame grill had best be of some correctly hued plastic or of attractive metal which will stand up against weather conditions and wear without taking on a "tarnish" to spoil the decorative scheme.

Some suggested latticed materials which come to mind are: galvanized chicken wire, brass or stainless steel mosquito mesh, decoratively punched radiator grill, woven or twisted fence grating, perforated plastic sheeting and plasticized netting. These may be lacquered or painted and left starkly bare or partially decorated by entwining materials or completely

Basic Shade & Frame Shapes..

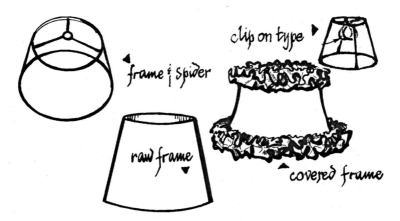

*frame & spider*

*clip on type*

*raw frame*

*covered frame*

covered with facing materials like cloths, plastic film or metal foil. It makes an interesting lampshade any way it is handled providing good taste is shown in the choice of colors, shapes and their combinations.

The fourth kind is the *cast* or *moulded* type. The lampshade or lamp-shield, whichever it may be, is cast in some material suitable to the functional structure of the lamp. As an illustration of this, suppose we consider a small pin-up lamp using a front shield or baffle piece as a shade. This might be made of a piece of clear waffle-surfaced thermoplastic resin which is heat-bent to curve around the lamp and attached to a double strap finger clamp which clips on or slips over the lamp socket for security. The waffled surface might have been factory moulded and would then come in a variety of such variegated surfaces. It might be either transparent or translucent. In either case the uneven surfaces of the plastic shield will diffuse the light sufficiently to eliminate all glare. There are casting plastics on the market which permit the craftsman to cast his own patterned-surface and pre-shaped lampshields, even to be able to imbed the metal attachments for clipping on to the sockets. Bathroom glass is an alternative material. This, if impossible to heat-bend, can be cut into panels and framed together. Smooth surfaced material is feasible if selected in highly colored hues to help break up the intense glare of the lamp.

Inverted shallow bowls cast in the opaque aqueous plastic materials make excellent night lampshades or for use on other small units. Here it may be modelled in plastilene, cast in a plaster of paris mold, then shell-cast in this water-resin. It has very little shrinkage, is strong though thin, may be colored to suit and takes a high gloss in buffing. The possibilities of this is great.

Somehow we should not forget the metal castings which may be used over the lumiline or short fluorescent desk lamps. These can be hitched to the back of the lamp support with adjustable screws then roll over, canopy-fashion to serve the lamp as shield or shade. Of course, one may construct it of sheet material if preferred. Repoussed design will help no end in decorating its surface as will many other popular techniques.

The variations of size and shape of each are based upon what place and function it is called upon to perform. In some small measure, the materials chosen will influence its form too.

# Methods of Shade Decoration

Lampshades may be made of many different materials, too numerous to include in this volume, and each material may be embellished and enhanced in scores of ways. In a general way, we shall explain the major techniques which are applicable to these. We shall sort these materials into arbitrary groups as closely resembling each other. The craftsman must make his own selection of shade and the method he chooses to decorate it, which, in his opinion, will artistically suit the special lamp needs.

## METAL

Painted decoration on opaque tin-plate shades is called "tole". These enjoyed great popularity during the French Directoire Period, even the Napoleonic Era. Sometimes the lampshade is made of some metal other than tin. Sheet iron, aluminum, dural, etc. are a few of the substitutes.

Normally, paint will not adhere evenly or permanently to a glossy metallic surface. Hence, it becomes necessary to prepare that surface for paint application to avoid flaking or peeling later. This shine or high gloss should be removed. The quickest way is to form a permanent chemical coat over the metal to serve as priming for the paint. Sheet iron and tin plate may be sponged with a vinegar solution. This will form a whitish covering over it. A very weak lye or any other "base" (hydroxide) solution will accomplish the same thing.

Now brush or spray a coat of colored lacquer or oil paint to cover the surface evenly. It should be noted here that the inside of the lampshade should be painted too, preferably in a light, bright or metallic paint to reflect as much of the light as possible. Over this base color many methods of specific decoration can be applied. Decal, decoupage, hand painting, stencil, silk screen, etc., are some which come to mind.

"Anodizing", the technique of applying dyes, not paint, to the surface of aluminum has proven to be pretty permanent. The surface of the metal is chemically treated to accept the dye along its surface. Where the metal has not been so prepared, the dye will have no effect upon it. It will simply wash off. The metal is then immersed into the dye bath and allowed to remain for a fixed time at a fixed temperature in order for the aniline dye to take. Once removed and dried, the metal can be buffed to a high gloss again and will retain its bright color for a considerable length of time under hard handling.

"Patina" coloring, a method of creating an antique finish on metals by use of chemicals and their reaction to these metals, is another technique. There are limited desired effects to be gotten in this manner and not too many metals can react to give interesting patinas. In any case, the metal must first be chemically clean. A quick rinse in a "pickling bath", a mild acid solution, followed by a water wash should do the job. The correct chemical is then brushed over the desired areas. The reaction is allowed to continue until it creates the color or tone you want. Wash off the chemical solution with water and you will fix it at that point. It may be repeated if needed. Since in many cases continued exposure to the atmosphere may bring on the reaction, it is suggested that a coating of water-clear metal lacquer be sprayed to cover the metal and prevent any possibility of such. See p. 88 for chart.

An imitative technique of getting these chemically "aged" results is "patina painting". In this the desired color effects are gotten with oil paint and brush. An undercoat of the metallic color is painted on first. After it is thoroughly dry, the antique coloring is applied by brush, then gently rubbed away from the highlight areas to give that time-polished effect.

The metal lampshade may of course be "tooled" to achieve one of two effects. One, to create a design by removing certain areas of the metal to permit the filtered light to contrast with the opacity of the lampshade material. Secondly, to get the design to show up against the flat surface of the metal by raising or lowering certain areas toward that end. These forms of decoration must be applied before the lampshade is assembled.

In the first case, "piercing" is the obvious method that comes to mind—piercing by punch, saw, knife, die cutter, etc. It is comparatively easy to scratch or cut through metals of thin gauge, but the heavier stock will require saws and punches to do the job properly. The second approach includes such techniques as repousse, stamping, scribing or drypoint-scratching, press-tooling, etching, etc. The amount which the metal is lowered or raised is immaterial, except in that it should look well with the decorative requirements of the rest of the lamp and the group in which it will take its place.

## WOOD

In the decorating processes of any material it is logical to figure the possible different approaches, then fit the individual technique into the proper group. For instance, when working on wood, we should investigate three possibilities: 1) decoration made on surface level, 2) that which can be incised or pierced below the surface, 3) designs applied to the surface causing it to rise above the level of it.

Let us examine the first approach. The lamp construction offers the craftsman a wood surface to be embellished. Here all methods of applying painted decoration on surface may be employed. There are the brush-on, spraying, pouncing, dipping, spattering, wipe-on, roll-on, off-set and dripping means of getting the paint on to the surface of the wood. It is well to note at this point that it may be more expedient in some cases to apply the decoration before the lampshade is assembled, in other situations it may not be feasible at all. It may be very much easier to manage one panel of the lampshade at a time when transferring a pattern of oil paint floating on water than maneuvering the cumbersome, assembled whole. It may be desired to keep the framing tape and lash-laces clean. The piece-meal approach solves this adequately.

The variations within this theme should prove interesting. A flat, solid coat of color is the most direct decoration. This may be applied with brush, spray-gun, by dipping it into a paint bath, wiping it on with a saturated cloth, or covering the surface, if flat, with an inked printer's brayer. The same can be applied when using stains and dyes instead of opaque paints, colored shellacs and lacquers. This does not preclude the use of clear varnish, shellac, wax and lacquer protective coverings.

On such undercoats more complex patterns can be applied. Transfer pictures like decalcomanias may be set-on, stencil units painted, "mono-type" offset prints set on directly from the plate or with a rubber roller large enough to carry the entire design, brush or wire-screen spattering, directed paint-dripping from a perforated can, patina-painting, are some of those which answer the description of "flat-surface" decoration. While inlay belongs in this group, it will be treated in greater detail later.

The second approach, the "intaglio" or below the surface decoration encompasses totally different techniques, many of which have been mentioned before in another section of the book, but not dwelled upon. The simplest of these is to scratch or cut incised lines to delineate a picture or design reminiscent of our "puppy-love" stage when mated initials mysteriously appeared very comfortably encased in a heart-shaped cartouche on the main street tree trunk, the local alley fence or the township school desk. Of course wood engraving is a more commercially developed "Mary-loves-John" technique.

Single or multiple point stipple biting into the wood's surface, whether applied by hand power or electric vibrating tools, offers a method of arranging pattern units by means of contrasting textural areas. These may later be tone-colored or painted in with various hues to further define the designs. Punches with preformed decorative units, much resembling the common number and letter punches, may be used in repeat order to construct a border or all-over pattern. This too may be stained to help accent the lower areas.

Fire, being another of man's tools, serves here too. Using a hot "poker" or an electric "pyro-pen", one can trace the contours of any pictorial decoration, even add tonal elements to create shading where necessary. Much along this same line, a gas or alcohol pressure torch can be played across a wooden surface which is partially shielded by a metal stencil to create a "charred or weather-worn" design. Much of this effect will depend upon the kind of wood grain used and the preliminary preparations and after-fire finish it is given. Experiment a bit before tackling any important job.

Should we try to dig below the "level of the skin", we could arrive at a decorative method like "chip carving". This is reminiscent of the cruder method of "nicking-out" letters and such with the point of the knife. Actually, it is the same excepting that now the design is planned and the motifs are geometric in spirit. Borders, panels and all-overs are the most popular theme here employed.

When we arrive at *intaglio carving*, we have merely released chip carving from its formalized shackles to roam with greater fluidity below the surface level. This is really low-relief carving, but that it is seen in reverse or negative form. It resembles a casting mold like the clay stamping blocks one sees in children's modelling toy sets.

*Routing* is basically a two-level drilling. More levels may be established if one is amply skilled to do so. This is done with a flat-pointed drill called a "router bit" which grinds and chews away selected areas leaving the remaining part raised. After smoothing with sandpaper, it may, like all carving be accentuated with chrome colors or tonal stains or else left in monotone and covered with a clear protective coating. In carrying this technique to the extreme, the designs should wind up as pierced through the entire thickness of the material. This may be done in a more direct manner by drilling strategic holes, then threading a coping saw blade through them enabling the pierced parts to be sawed away. Any other method of cutting through is still called *piercing*.

The last method of decorative treatment implied that the design be raised above the surface of the material. This differs from the intaglio method even though in cutting the surface down a high area remains which may even be the motif itself, it is nevertheless not any higher than the original surface was in the beginning. In this *relief* approach, the motif is actually raised or built up higher than the starting surface. The one exception to this is the *carved* design, both of *high* and *low* relief. Here we deliberately begin with a thicker piece of wood, thick enough to cover the highest point of the sculptured area then the background is routed down to a level it might have been had the carved part been superimposed upon that level.

Wood may be treated with *appliques* of other decorative items and units. Thin wood silhouettes and fret cut-outs may be glued to the surface at select points to form the lampshade decoration. Whether in contrasting or like color, these become relief decoration. Metal nailheads, synthetic wood, plastic or metal mold-castings can serve as mounted decoration. In fact, molding strips may be fastened as lattice, fretted or border designs on the lampshade surface.

*Laminates* of thin plastic material, decorative papers, fabrics, leather are of the raised type of shade treatment, although limited in height due to the nature of the added material. A *montage* is a laminate where many pictures are cut and pasted in juxtaposed position over the surface to cover it in a smooth layer.

When a thin film of wood is used to cover the entire surface perhaps to get a selected grain or color, it is called *veneer*. Should the original sur-

face be completely covered with such layers of wood but contour-cut and matched to form a vary-decorative surface, that is called *marquetry*.

If, however, contour pieces of different woods are inserted into gouged-out sections to form a design against the background of the original wood, that is known as inlay. Most often these inlaid pieces rise to the same level as the background, but often as not it might rise higher than that. When bone, ivory, stone or plastics are substituted for wood as inlay material, it is known as "certosina". These, among the innumerable variations and combinations, are outstanding ways of decorating wood in relief.

## PAPER

When paper is used as the cover material for the lampshade, it must be remembered that a great deal of specification enters even in the description of the word "paper". Usually, it is not to be expected that the "common, garden-variety" of paper is inferred. Most often it is some novelty product or if one of the more usual types, it is probably so specially treated that it can well be considered in the novelty group.

Examine the catalogues of the larger paper manufacturing firms or wholesale houses and you will discover scores of such products as will serve your almost every need of paper for lampshade covering. In addition to this vast variety new numbers are constantly being prepared and released to the ever-hungry public.

The same manner of decorative group will hold here as it did with wood. Piercing, which may, incidentally, be done with a sharp knife or razor blade, is one of the intaglio means. Others are cardboard carving, punching with hole or needle punches and any other technique of perforation. The raised or relief methods list such as over-lay pasting, montage, decoupage, flocking in which the whole or part of the surface is covered with an adhesive layer on to which is sprinkled or blown short, cut fibers which will stick to those areas. It creates a furry-textural effect. Other materials may be adhered as decorative treatment like fine colored sand, spangle and glitter sprinkle.

The greatest group is that which conforms to surface treatment. All the better known painting forms as oil, tempera, water color painting, crayon coloring, tinting, dyeing, antiqueing, spatter-work, pen and ink sketching, pencil, lithograph drawing, fingerpainting, gouache painting, decals, press-ons and other transfer pictures. In the print division, one recognizes such

techniques as silk screen, stencil prints, photography, photostats, solar and blueprints. Even mimeograph and ditto gelatin prints are accepted in this group. It goes without question that etching, drypoint, messo-tint, monotype, colotype and lithograph prints fit this bill of definition. A growing enthusiasm for coated and impregnated stock makes it mandatory to at least mention these varieties. The most common is oil-soaking the paper, giving it a parchment-like quality. Plastics serve as a soaking solution and as a spray doing double duty as desired. The various gums and lac derivatives function in a similar manner making them equally desirable. In all of this, it must be assumed that color can be added in the process to further enhance the paper product.

## SKINS AND LEATHERS

Skins should include the entire group of leathers, hides, furs gotten from the animal, bird, reptile and fish families. Some of these have inherent color and decorative markings leaving only the curing process to be applied before making it ready for use. Some leathers require coloring as well as tanning and some whose pliability and texture is such that it can be pressed and tooled to create decorative scoring on their surfaces.

With this material as with those which preceded, many of the accepted techniques are applicable. It may be stained or painted. In fact, when given successive coats of lacquer and rubbed down smoothly after each coat has hardened, the leather becomes known as "patent leather". Then, too, it may be stencilled, sprayed and all the other plano-surface treatments. Punching, carving, underlaying, scraping (skiving), stamping, tooling and perforating can be used with which to create designs in the leather. The relief methods run about the same as usual. Relief modelling which is done just like the repousse on metal, from the wrong side upward, is the most outstanding extreme method. It moves down the line to applique pieces which are either rubber cemented to the background or sewn (stitched) on. Nailheads and buttons are additional dressing pieces which can be used to embellish leather goods.

## TEXTILES AND FABRICS

Within the textile group the largest division applicable for use on lampshades is the fabrics family. Let us examine this more closely. All fabrics are made when vertical threads (warp) are interlaced with horizontal

ones (weft). When this interlacing is simply over and under, each line alternating with the thread line above, it results in a *plain* weave. If the horizontal thread covers two vertical threads, then follows under two and repeats, we have a *twill* weave which creates an oblique line effect. Have the horizontal thread cross over three weft threads and under one then repeat, it results in a satin weave. In this, cloth is made by weaving or knitting fibers together. The manner in which these threads are interlaced produces different weaves. It is the texture and pattern created by these weaves that makes for the ever-expanding horizons and the wide scope of interest derived from cloth. Couple this with the numerous colors of threads and their possibilities of combination. It is enough to stagger even the wildest imagination.

Still further multiplication of possibilities is developed by the nature of the materials used and in the finishing of the fabrics. Most common among the threads are cotton, wool, silk, linen, mohair (hair), ramie, jute (plant), and such plastic fibers as rayon, cellophane, nylon, saran, vinyl, even such minerals as metallic thread and asbestos. The finishing includes bleaching, dyeing, shrinking, sponging, loading, printing and all kinds of special processes like batik, crinkling, moire, etc. This gives a small view of the infinite variety which fabrics can offer.

Even after the fabric has been woven, such processes as embroidery, crewel work, quilting, tufting, tieing and dyeing, silk-screening, stencilling, coating and impregnating can be applied to alter the appearance of the material.

## FIBERS

In close relation with fabrics stands the fibers themselves. These are gotten from the same animal, mineral, plant and synthetic source as those used for cloth. However, when used as fiber, they have a totally different appeal. These may be used in single strand, twisted, wound or braided to perform the task it is called upon to do. Tassels, fringe, braided cords and lash-lace are some of the purposes it may serve. Because it lacks body and substance, it must have some sort of frame over which it can be wound, wrapped or entwined.

Some of the hardier wood fibers like reed, rope, rattan, raffia, bamboo strips, etc. can be woven into hat and basket forms which can easily be converted into novelty lampshades and lampshields. These are usually

sprayed, painted or dyed to get needed hues introduced into the end result
—the lampshade.

## PLASTICS

There are some natural *plastic* materials like wax, rubber, gelatin, tar
and paraffin. But for the most part, the public is best acquainted with the
synthetic resin division of plastics. Let us then consider just that group.
To the uninformed, all plastics are alike especially if they are colorless
and transparent. There is nothing further from the truth than that state-
ment.

Basically, there are seven major synthetic family groups and within
each group many variations, many sufficiently different in appearance, that
it is difficult to reconcile their relationship. These groups are: the phenols
(made of formaldehyde), the aminos (made of the ureas), the acrylics
(lucite and plexiglas), the styrenes, the cellulosic (cellulose derivative),
the vinyls and the proteins (casein, etc.).

All of the above divide into two classes. The first two, the phenols and
aminos, are called *thermoset* plastics because once they have become hard
in the process of heat-curing, heat will no longer affect it—certainly not
be able to soften it. The rest of them belong to the *thermoplast* group.
Here, even though it took heat to harden it to solidity, if heated again it
will soften sufficiently to be bent and re-shaped.

To clearly understand this phenomenon, let us compare the thermo*set* to
an egg omelet and the thermo*plast* to gelatin dessert. The omelet solidifies
when heated, but once hard, no matter how much or how long it is continued, the heat will have no other effect but to char or burn it. So it is
with thermoset. With gelatin, however, after it has been heated and allowed
to harden, it will soften once heated again. Too much heat or applied for
too long will "burn" the gelatin as will happen with the thermoplastic
resin. It is interesting to note that when a thermoplast is heated to a pliable
state then bent into some other shape, and finally to cool into fixed form,
it will so remain. But should it ever be subjected to sufficient heat, enough
to make it flexible again, it will twist back to its original shape if nothing
prevents it from adjusting itself. This is a sort of *plastic memory.*

Thermoplasts offer the greatest possibilities for craft work because it
*can* be shaped after it has been presented for commercial sale. The thermosets are more limited, but have properties of hardness and resistance to

| PLASTIC FAMILIES | | |
| --- | --- | --- |
| | THERMO | |
| 1. Phenol | Set | 1. Phenol Formaldehyde |
| 2. Amino (Urea) | Set | Phenol Furfural |
| 3. Acrylic | Plast | Urea Formaldehyde |
| 4. Styrene | Plast | Metamine Methacrylate |
| 5. Cellulosic | Plast | 3. Methyl Methacrylate |
| 6. Vinyl | Plast | 4. Polysterene |
| 7. Protien | Plast | 5. Cellulose Nitrate |
| | | Cellulose Acetate |
| | | Cellulose Acetate-Butyrate |
| | | 6. Vinyl Chloride-Acetate |
| | | Vinylidene Chloride |
| | | 7. Polyamide |
| | | Casein |

heat which are most favorable.

Let us examine the scope of working with these materials. It can be bought in powdered or liquid form from which state it may be cast or molded then cured. The "set resins" offer greater possibilities here. The "plasts" shrink too much as a rule.

In *casting*, thermosetting materials are poured as liquids, the powdered material is first liquefied, poured into molds and hardened with a baking process afterward. The *molding* processes are less likely to be feasible as a home or small shop activity, hence it is mentioned only in passing. Even the use of thermoplasts in *blow* or *vacuum* molding is hardly advised for small shop manufacture. In this operation "plasts" are formed like glass blowing in hot molds forcing air or steam between to heated sheets of resin and forcing them against the mold walls.

*Lamination* of layers of other kinds of sheet material bonded together into a solid body can be done on an individual and small scale. Here thermoset casting materials might be used as impregnating and bonding agents.

Plastic materials are available in many basic forms. They are rolled in *sheets* of varied thickness and surface textures, extruded in assorted-sized *moldings, tubes,* and *rods,* prefabricated in *decorative units* as might be suited for use as lamp finials and switch plates, and produced as *threads* of all diameters. Fantastic predictions have been made about the replacement value plastics has for metal, wood, glass and leather, but this is hardly so. There are limited overlapping areas, to be sure, but for the most part all these materials are mutually exclusive. Many partnerships have developed between such materials as in the textile coating, the bonding and laminating markets (safety glass and plywood), in the display and container industries, and in the paint and glue fields. But mainly, their growth has been in individual directions along a common path.

Once having this material, it is well that we know how to work with it. This should answer specific questions of procedure as it progresses.

In the *forming* and *shaping* operations, we have the most common—*sawing*. Only the rigid plastics should be sawed. The cutting teeth should be filed to a vertical or slight back-rake and not coarser than 12 or 14 point. Flat cutting is preferable to end cutting for straight line work. A coping or jeweler's saw frame is recommended for intricate shapes. Slow strokes and constant clearing of sawdust will prevent "burning" of the plastics. Thermoplasts burn quicker than thermoset materials. Power saws should be refiled to have this negative tooth rake and above all use a slower speed with plenty of "coolant" either as water, air or tallow-bar supply. Avoid the slightest feel of force-feeding the material into the machine. Keep vibration at a minimum.

Thermoplastic materials are more adaptable to *shearing* than the others. This can be done with any tool from a small pair of scissors to a large paper cutter or bench shears, providing it can accommodate the thickness of the material. Avoid splitting and cracking by preheating the plastic to its "flabby-point". At that temperature a knife can slice it like butter.

While *turning* is hardly a likely operation for lampshade making, it should be mentioned in passing. It may be done on a wood or a metal lathe, but mounting the material must be solved in light of the job to be done, the form of the material to be turned and the machine at hand. The speeds and techniques compare with those used on bessemer steel or brass. *Milling* and *shaping* must be handled with the same precautions that apply to handling of brass.

The *bending* processes, which are heat-applying techniques, are compatible to thermoplastic materials. Most plastics can be softened sufficiently at temperatures below 212 degrees Fahrenheit. This makes it convenient to immerse the piece into a pot of boiling water, hold it there for several minutes, and bend it (preferably in jigs) immediately upon removal. Since plastic resinoids are poor heat conductors, it is possible to heat-bend a section at a time wtihout affecting the rest of it. Several types like the acrylics or the styrenes require higher temperatures and dry heat. It is then suggested that an electric hot plate, an asbestos pad over a flame, or an infra-red lamp be used to supply such heat. Once bent to the desired form, it must be kept that way until it has cooled sufficiently throughout its thickness to remain rigid. It may be aided by passing air or water over it although this is apt to cause undue strains and stresses within the material. Arcs and radial bends of less than 10% of the thickness of the material are extremely hazardous. Jigs and preforms must be completely arranged before the work is removed from the heat source in order that it be formed within the shortest period possible. Simple bends may be done by finger pressure and eye judgment. It is wise to wear gloves while handling the hot materials.

The *assembly* operations follow after all parts have been properly cut and bent to proper size and shape. Many methods suggest themselves, some having greater technical advantage than others, but the choice lies with the craftsman who must be aware of as many of these operational possibilities.

*Cementing* should be used where a firm bond is necessary between plastic surfaces. The pieces must fit accurately and be clean for the best results in joint construction. Wherever possible, it is best to cement flat surfaces than curved ones, hence the advice to route or sand "flats" to create such surfaces. The matching parts should be smooth, though not necessarily polished except where transparent joints are required. The entire principle of cementing of plastics is based upon the actual *cohesion* of the material itself, although there are several glues that have very strong *adhesive* qualities and may be used for a temporary joint. Thermosets are treated differently from the thermoplast resinoids. The entire cementing process resolves itself into three possibilities: 1) joining thermoset to thermoset, 2) thermoset to thermoplast, and 3) thermoplast to thermoplast.

**83**

In the first place, the best cement to use is the raw resinoid base as cement. Practically every manufacturer of cast resins and thermosetting plastics produces such products in cement form. This is simply the resin not yet cured or polymerized. In order to harden this kind of cement, it must be subjected to dry heat at about 200 degrees Fahrenheit for about 12 hours. This time may be shortened by using catalysts like hydrochloric acid or those specially prepared by the manufacturer for that purpose. When this cement is cured, it is worked in the same manner as the material itself.

The second combination of joining "set to plast" it is well to consider them both as thermosetting materials and treat them accordingly.

When adhering thermoplast to thermoplast, a new line of procedure is followed. Here we try to soften the matching faces and have them intermingle so there is the same cohesion as in the rest of the material, molecule to molecule. It resembles the "melting and freezing action" accomplished when two pieces of metal are welded together.

Soak, dip or paint the touching parts with an organic *solvent* of the material. If the same thermoplasts are used, it is comparatively easy. If they are different, then the corresponding solvents must be used for each. When strength is unimportant, press together the "cushions", made by this softening process. To create greater permanence add a viscous cement, as might be commercially prepared or as might be made when shavings of plastics are dissolved in the solvent to thicken it to the correct viscosity. The successful joint again requires: 1) an accurate and clean fit, 2) the proper "preparation" of the surfaces, and 3) the proper pressure applied for the proper length of time.

It is quite possible to fuse two thermoplastic resins by the judicious use of heat and pressure. When bringing the plastic surface in contact with a very hot metal surface, it becomes semi-liquid—soft and wet. If two such surfaces are brought together with sufficient pressure for them to intermingle, they will form a bond almost as strong as the original material. If cooled too rapidly, however, the material will shrink unevenly, set up severe stresses, form a brittle joint and tend to "craze". A variety of heating elements may be used from an electric soldering iron to a pressing (flat) iron. The techniques depend upon the type of joint, the strength required and the individual ingenuity of the craftsman. This is the *heat weld* joint.

Occasionally the need arises when *riveting* must be used, especially when other holding devices do not work, or plastics must be joined to other materials like metal, glass or wood. Soft metal rivets fit the bill best and escutcheon pins may be substituted for small-sized rivets. Countersink the back of the hole to provide for the spread and swell of the rivet during the hammering process. This will avoid "feathering" around the hole. If amply countersunk, the rivet may be headed into the plastic, then filed flush with the surface.

A variation of the rivet which combines with the strength of a thread is the *drive screw*. This is used particularly where a permanent joint is intended, sufficient thickness of material is available so that the rivet shall not "escape" through the back. Drill a hole through the layer of plastic adjacent to the head of the rivet to allow it to slip through easily but not loosely. Drill an undersized, matching hole into the second layer of material to act as a "pilot". Drill this a little deeper than needed to accommodate any air or dust trapped inside. Hold the two parts of the plastic firmly together, then drive the screw down with a series of light taps until every part holds snugly together.

When necessary, *self-tapping screws* can be substituted for rivets or drive screws. This is obviously necessary when the joined parts must be taken apart at intervals. These are inserted in the same manner as are inserted with a screw driver instead of a hammer.

*Drilling* in plastics is not unlike drilling into soft metals. The regular machine twist drill bits may be used, but they have a tendency to "hog in" or "grab" the shavings as with lead and aluminum to clog the cutting flutes of the bit. Special highly polished, straight-shanked and straight-fluted soft metal drill bits may be used with greater success. Hole saws and fly-cutters should be used for holes larger than one inch in diameter.

A lubricant, such as a mild soap solution or mineral oil, should be used as a coolant unless a constant air-jet feed at the point of drilling is available. Frictional heat accumulates as the drill penetrates deeply. Therefore, remove the drill bit every half-inch of drilling depth to clear out the chips and to re-lubricate. Remove the drill bit from the material while it is still in motion to prevent it from "freezing" in the hole.

*Tapping* and *threading* are done with standard taps and dies, using the large (2 or 3) flutes to help clear out the chips. Follow the same precautions as is used for drilling. Avoid unnecessarily fine threads, the fracture rate of such threads is great.

*Internal carving*, another name for drill-engraving in clear plastics, utilizes a pointed and tapered drill bit especially made for such purpose. Here, the various strokes are drilled from the reverse side of the plastics to be seen from the front. A little practice should help to determine the different methods of twisting the moving bit to get special effects and results like petals, leaves, stems, buds, etc.

In searching for methods and materials in applying *decoration* to the plastic body, the craftsman has seen fit to invade the kindred fields of design. Painting, printing, sculpture, industrial design and mechanics have subscribed or been drafted to assist. Once the plastic job has been formed, it requires some kind of surface decoration. The simplest attention it can get is a high gloss finish. Here all scratches are removed by rubbing it with a "slush" made of powdered pumice or flour of rottenstone with water. This results in a satin-like finish comparable to *frosting* and may be left at that point. To get it to a high-luster finish, it must be rubbed with such greasebound compounds as Tripoli, Learock, Plascore or Wilco Polishing Compound. Apply this with light but continuous pressure. This *buffing* is often the final operation. However, a coat of hand-rubbed paste or emulsified wax will protect the surface and fill in tiny hair scratches to render them less apparent.

Where color was not originally put into the plastic "mix" when it was manufactured, it might be added by means of a surface dye. This technique involves the complete dipping of the part in a dye bath and left in it for the length of time required to get the depth of color wanted. These dyes are usually anilines dissolved in water or alcohol and applied to clear plastics. A hot dye bath will penetrate deeper into the material than a cold bath will.

Hand *painted* decorations may be applied with opaque oil paints, enamel paints lack body for coverage, in the same manner as it is used on wood, canvas or metal. Priming is not needed. Concentrated dyes or plastic pigment paint can be brushed on to create decorative patterns. In a like manner, *stencil* designs or *silk-screen* pictures might be pounced,

| NATURAL PLASTICS | | SYNTHETIC PLASTICS |
|---|---|---|
| **THERMOPLASTICS** | | |
| Rosin | Waxes | Ethyl Methacrylate |
| Shellac | Paraffins | Polystrene |
| Copals | Rubber Latex | Cellulose (Acetate, Nitarate) |
| Asphalt | Glue | Cellulose Acetate-Butyrate |
| Bitumens | Tar | Ethyl Cellulose |
| Amber | Coumarone | Vinyl Chloride Acetate |
| | | Vinylidane Chloride |
| **THERMOSETS** | | |
| Casein | | Phenol Formaldehyde |
| Gelatin | | Phenol Furfural |
| Shellac (with catalyst) | | Urea Formaldehyde |
| Coumarone-Indene | | Melamine Formaldehyde |
| Lignan | | |

brushed, sprayed or squeegeed on plastic.

*Printing* may be done on plastic surfaces from blocks of all kinds including type. The material should be warmed to prevent cracking or breakage when undue pressure might be applied. *Offset printing* is a variation of the above assuring complete safety from breakage. The picture is printed on cloth, rubber or some gelatin plate and while the ink is still wet, the transfer plate is pressed against the plastic surface thereby setting off the wet, printed design. Transfer pictures like *decalcomanias* are a variation of this type of offset. Substituting for this, one can use *picture paste-ons*. Photographs, magazine cut-outs or other kinds of printed pictures are cut out in silhouette and cemented in position. A protective coating of lacquer or plastic spray will help protect it. This is more commonly known as *decoupage*. Such overlays serve well and permanently.

*Electroplating* may be done on plastics even though resinoids are nonconductors of electricity. If first coated with flake graphite, those areas will take electroplating. Mix the graphite with a binder and paint it on.

Suppose we soften the thermoplastic material, then press a hot metal stamp into it, the replica design of the stamp will be impressed by this *branding* method. If a piece of thin metal foil is placed between the branding iron and the plastic, a *metallic imprint* will result.

Pictures may be scratched into the plastic surface with a knife or needle point to get designs. Crayon and paints of all kinds and colors may be rubbed into these *scribed* lines to accent the decoration. Finer line quality can be gotten by using an engraver's burin in much the same way that metal is *engraved*. Warm the plastics to avoid chipping. Relief and intaglio *carving* turns to the sculptor's field and can be very effective where the thickness of the material permits. If not, cameo pieces may be cemented onto the surface of the lampshade itself.

When working with paper-thin stock, it is well to refer to the section on paper and adapt many of the decorative techniques like jack knife carving, punch designs, underlays and montage pasting to plastics.

# GLASS

The use of glass for lampshades and light shields are limited to those which can give it adequate structural support since most of the decorative

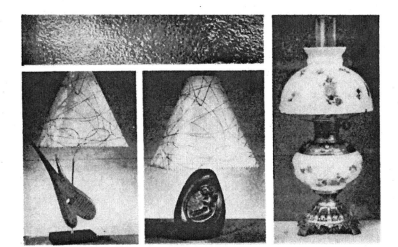

forms of sheet stock runs thick and, therefore, heavy and to the style of design which is compatible with the decorative effect limited to glass.

We shall consider the glass commercially made and marketed before we explore the workshop techniques of glass decoration. There is a very large group of precast and moulded glass which vary in particular size and specifically *figured*, *textured* and *ornamental* surface with the company which manufactures it. Some of the trade titles they are described as very as do these; chipped, corrugated, crinkled, embossed, hammered, louvred, pebbled, prismed (plain and interlaced), reeded, ribbed, roughed, tapestry, and waffled. These are translucent and do a remarkable job of diffusing the light.

A variation of this is the *wired glass* in which the embedded interlaced wire creates the ornamental embellishment of the glass. In this, the wire of polished or dull metal is either twisted or welded to form the mesh.

Another large group falls under the classification of smooth-surfaced, *polished glass*. Besides being available in clear, transparent stock, it is manufactured in assorted solid colors and in novelty color variations. It may be made in transparent or translucent hues with the entire thickness of glass so *colored* or with just a partial layer *stained* on one or both sides. This latter kind may be ground through the layer to expose a two-tone design. It may be *opal* colored, *marbleized* and in *iridescent* tones. Of course, overall frosted finishes are not unknown just as it might be mirror-silvered. Frosting can be made by rubbing the surface with a carborundum and oil "sludge-paste". Decorative frosting may be imitated by sandblasting the glass through a metal stencil or applying the commercial etching paste instead. The tried and true method of waxing the glass surface, scratching away a design, then holding face downward over hydrofluoric acid for its fumes to "etch" into the exposed parts is a bit risky. The acid is very volatile and poisonous and should *not* be attempted unless by an experienced person.

*Gray carvings* of intricacy are feasible with a motor-driven grinding wheel. Trace the design on the front with a china marking pencil, then grind the markings on the reverse side. When these designed areas are cut deeply and polished again, it becomes "cut glass" or *polished carving*.

**87**

## PATINAS

| METAL | COLORING SOLUTION | RESULTING COLORS |
|---|---|---|
| Aluminum<br>Brass | 1. Caustic soda, then nitric acid. | Blanching |
| | 2. Arsenic and iron dissolved in HCl. | Black |
| | 3. Olive oil and heated. | Brown to black |
| |    or brush. | Copper plate |
| | 4. Copper sulphate, cream of tartar, sodium hydroxide in water solution. Dip | Orange to black |
| | 5. Water sol. of potassium, sodium or ammonium sulphate. | Black |
| | 6. Heat in air to oxidize. | Browns |
| | 7. Potassium chlorate and copper sulphate. | Violet and blue |
| | 8. Copper sulphate, sodium hyposulphite and cream of tartar. | Red, blue, pale |
| | 9. Orpiment, and crystallized sal sodas. |    lilac to white |
| | 10. Cream of tartar and copper sulphite. | Iridescent |
| | 11. Copper carbonate and caustic soda. | Yellow to |
| | 12. Copper acetate, copper sulphate and alum. |    bright red |
| | 13. Arsenic chloride or sodium hyposulphite. | Green |
| | 14. Sodium hydrate, copper carbonate. | Steel blue to blue |
| | 15. Dip in $H_2SO_4$ and $HNO_3$ containing zinc sulphate. | Greenish brown |
| Bronze<br>Copper<br>Iron<br>Silver<br>Steel | 16. Same as for Brass. | Marbleized |
| | 17. Same as in Brass or Bronze #1-#16. |    blood-bronze |
| | 18. Sprinkle borax on red-hot surface of metal. | Orange |
| | 19. Dip in crystalized copper acetate. | Crystal violet |
| | 20. Antimony chloride plus mild heat in cp. sulphate. | Pale green |
| | 21. Sal ammoniac in vinegar. Add alum and arsenic. | Metallic moire |
| | 22. Cream of tartar, copper sulphate plus "hypo." | |
| | 23. "Hypo" solution and lead acetate solution boiled. | Blue |
| | 24. Mix ($NH_4Cl$) salt with mercury and water. Immerse "red" heated metal. | Silver white |
| | 25. Silver chloride in "hypo." Add $NH_4Cl$. Rub on metal till dry. | Silver |
| | 26. Dilute sulphuric acid saturate with iron oxide. | Gold tint |
| | 27. Dilute nitric acid bath. Rinse in cyanide pot. | Frosted |
| | 28. Bismuth chloride, bichloride of mercury chloride, hydrochloric acid, alcohol. Dip or brush on. | Black |
| | 29. Iron chloride, solid antimony chloride, gallic acid and water. Sponge on 3 coats. Dry in air. | Blue |
| | 30. Copper sulphate, spirits of niter and distilled water. | Brown |
| | 31. Dip in hydrochloric acid, wash, immerse in hot alcohol. | Blanch |

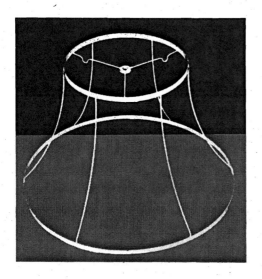

# Constructing a Lampshade

The process of making a lampshade follows a four step routine which involves: first the planning, secondly collecting or making of all parts, third putting these parts together and last, decorating and adding the finish to it. In the initial step, the decision of which size and shape is most suitable for the need it must fulfill, the selection of proper materials for the task and the patterns called for are made. The second phase is purely one of technique involving the use of the materials selected for the job. The third part of this development entails the assembling of parts according to plan. This is self-explanatory and will be filled in with greater detail wherever the specific need occurs. The final step involves the coloring, decorating and protecting of the surfaces as required by the lamp plans. In some cases, the color is inherent in the materials used so that it is being dealt with earlier when the parts are being laid out and cut. For example, when selecting a fabric for the lampshade, it is necessary to make the choice of color, even decorative design on the fabric, while selecting the textile. This does not disprove the logic of following these steps. It simply proves that their sequence may overlap each other a bit.

Let us construct a lampshade for a typical lamp in each of the major groups we have outlined previously. This we will take as a step-by-step project to illustrate the technique of planning, shaping parts, assembling the parts and finishing the lamp. Alternate suggestions should grow on the basis of these principles. Combinations and additional ideas are up to the reader's creativeness. Carrying out of these ideas obviously becomes one of need, opportunity, technical skill and influence of costs.

# $\mathcal{P}_{art}$ IV
## $\mathcal{L}amps$ and $\mathcal{L}ampshades$

# Table Pedestal Lamp

## LAMPSHADE

Plastic material comes in many forms—in solid sheets, bars, rods, etc., in films, and in various degrees of viscosity as liquids. Such liquids can span open areas up to twenty square inches. Framing members made of wire should be constructed and dipped into this viscous material. Its cohesive quality causes this material to fasten itself firmly over the structural outline while the surface tension of the material itself causes it to span the intervening openings as a tightly-drawn film. Upon drying through evaporation, this film becomes a strong, firm material, having the strength and rigidity of cellophane—when increased in thickness, it will become stronger. The lampshade herein detailed is intended to fit the pedestal lamp base previously described.

The top and bottom squares are made of $3/8'' \times 3/32''$ semi-hard flat brass stock. In order to get a sharp right angle bend, cut halfway through the inside flat before bending. Tap lightly and evenly to prevent fracturing the material. File a mitred joint where the two ends meet and braze or sweat-solder the junction.

Join both these metal square loops with a $9\frac{1}{2}''$ #8 semi-hard brass wire. Braze or solder them to the appropriate inside corners of each loop. Add another such wire rib amidship of each side of the top and bottom loops. One inch to the left and one to the right of each of these midribs, solder a wire that is bent to cross the top and follow back as an adjoining rib of the next side of the shade, see diagram. Covering the top corner areas, solder an 8'' square of copper mesh mosquito wire. When dipped, this will give the effect of a sparkle surface plastic insert.

Attach the $4\frac{1}{2}''$ disc so that it joins up all the intersecting ribs that appear across the top of the shade. Add a 1'' brass washer over the center of this plate and drill the hole through. Polish and buff all the metal parts so that they will remain bright under the protective coating of the liquid plastic material.

Now the shade is immersed into a vat of viscous plastic span liquid and tilted so that the excess resin will run off to leave an even film. This viscous material spans all surface between the metal ribs just as soap film would form when a child's bubble-making loop is immersed into lathered water. Allow it to harden and you will find that it results in a clear, transparent, firm film of sufficient strength to make its handling reasonably safe. A harder and heavier film can be achieved by spraying or redipping the shade with overcoat sealing plastics.

Dyes and opaque paints may be procured to paint the inside of the various areas with appropriate colors. Plastic pigments are those which will give a wide variety of effects such as a crystal texture, a phosphorescence, a pearl iridescence, etc. Plan the color scheme of the shade to suit the needs of the room and the unit upon which it will be placed, then follow it carefully. This will reduce error to a minimum for it is practically impossible to remove the paint once applied. When this is done and the paint is dried sufficiently, a fixing medium is sprayed to render the colors permanent.

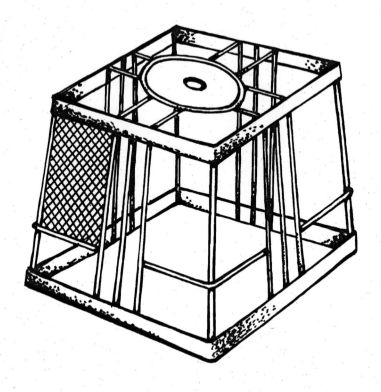

## BASE

Lamp bases are a more constant factor than the lampshade. Shades may be recovered, altered or replaced, but the base invariably remains. It is only when major redecorative surgery is applied to the room, or when a complete change of scheme is involved that lamp bases are replaced.

These stands have been made of many materials; wood, metal, ceramic, stone, glass, etc., so why not of plastic material. Belt buckle cast or extruded stock is used. In this case it is brown, square, smooth-surfaced, combined with round, fluted ivory colored plastic material. To avoid the monotony of texture, a decorative square base is purchased for it at any electrical supply house. These plastic buckle bars are cut to sizes indicated in the stock bill. These parts now constitute the major height of the pedestal base.

Assemble all parts in the order shown in the diagram starting with the lock nut under the metal base which threads on the electrical pipe up to the lamp socket set within the harp. Attach the double twisted strand lamp cord to the binding posts of this socket and lead it through the center of the electrical pipe, then out from the lead-hole in the base. End this extension wire with a male plug. Do this before you screw all parts firmly together.

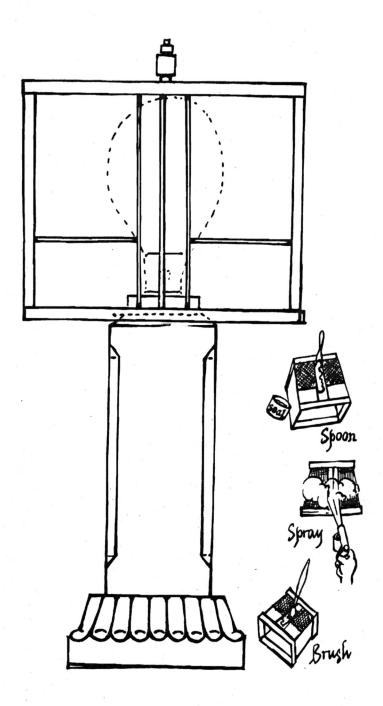

Spoon

Spray

Brush

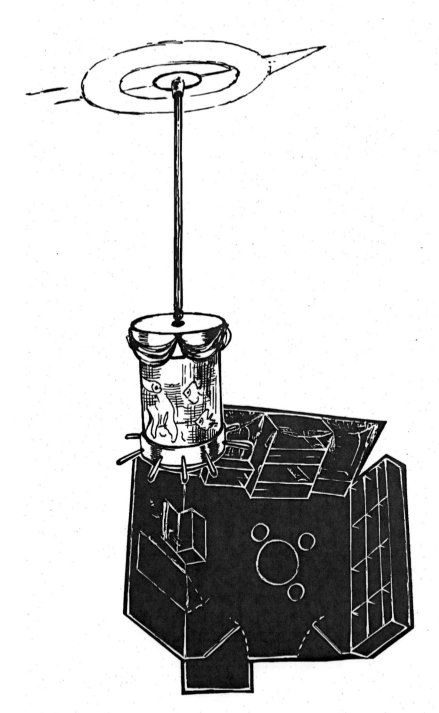

# Pendant Ceiling Light

Let us suppose we need a ceiling light for a child's room. Within this room we have the following influences which might affect the final form of this lamp. It is a boy's room, a boy about 10 or 12 years of age. This boy's preference runs towards ships and things nautical. The room, about twelve feet square, has a ten foot ceiling. It contains a double bunker bed with pin-up binnacle lights along each forward poster. This bed is set between two high windows. Sea-chest window-seats are beneath them and a valance of heavy fishing net hangs across the room above these windows and the topmost posts of the bunker beds.

The wall next to it has 6 foot shelves stretching in an unbroken line across the room. These are topped with models of sea-going vehicles.

The wall opposite this is broken by a door leading into the bathroom and flanked by a Governor Winthrop drop-leaf desk. This is fronted by a Windsor or rush-seated, ladder-back chair. Above the desk hangs a large treasure map with a parchmented wall bracket light fastened along either side of it.

The fourth wall contains the entrance door balanced by the closet door on its right. Between them may be a bracket console with a mirror above it. Directly in the center of the room is a three or four foot circular pedestal table with three or four chairs straddling it. It is above this table that the ceiling outlet appears from which a fixture should extend.

Three ideas immediately suggest themselves. They are: 1) a recessed circular fixture to resemble a porthole with its swing door; 2) a circular flush fixture which may be made to look like a ship's compass; 3) a pendant fixture extending four feet below the ceiling level to show a main theme of a ship's steering wheel. Let the latter one be that which we will develop. These are the reasons:

We need a great deal of general, diffused illumination within the room. This is more easily accomplished by suspending a "boom" light to a position somewhere within the volume of the room than by means of a lamp set high. Greater efficiency is possible. We can also arrange to cast direct light directly upon this circular table through an opening in the bottom of the lamp. This may be magnified with a Fresne lens inserted to form a spotlight. The open area at the top of this fixture makes it possible to spill a good deal of the otherwise wasted direction of the beams upon the ceiling area. This will add to the diffused illumination of a general nature. The sides of this pendant fixture may be made of translucent material which can permit as much light through as you'd care to allow. This can be controlled to create color notes which may build up the atmosphere and mood of the room towards its logical goal. In all, this pendant lamp serves a triple purpose. It sets up diffused general lighting to permit the unhampered activity of the room; it supplies direct lighting over the prescribed area of operation and aids the decorative and illusionary nature of the entire room design. Therefore, we chose this lamp.

# Bracket Wall Fixture

This lamp is an improvement over the turn-of-the-century gas jets in both appearance and efficiency. Though it has taken on unprecedented forms through modern design and engineering, even become part of the architectural structure rather than the adopted piece of ornamental wall trim, it remains to a great extent, an accepted necessity in most small homes of traditional design. Suppose we seek a wall lamp fixture which will suit the needs of an 18th Century American dining room. A pair of these lamps are suggested to flank the buffet sideboard, to lend the proper air and some authenticity. Neither the furniture nor the furnishings are of early colonial or provincial style. It therefore rates elegance. Since the buffet sideboard suggests dining and serving, what is more appropriate than to convert a platter and a cup and saucer into lamp to identify its place in the room. One might use an extra matching piece of the household service china. However, it is not out of place to choose an individual piece.

These brackets can be made of identical platters and identical cups and saucers, but it is still within good taste—in fact it would prove an interesting variation, to use mated pieces. They may be identical in shape and vary in decoration or vary in shape though similar in decoration. Any of these combinations, if selected in close harmony, should be recognized as a "mated pair."

Drill a hole through the center of the plate, the saucer and the bottom of the cup. Use a triangular file ground to a 45 degree angle point in a hand brace while the point of this home made bit is bathed in a sludge made of emery dust in kerosene and walled in by a clay bank. Slow, careful grinding will lap-grind a hole through. Avoid using excess pressure on the brace. It will crack or break the delicate chinaware.

Bend a piece of electrical pipe threaded on both ends, one end to a "U" curve with a six inch diameter, and the other end to a 90 degree curve in the opposite direction. Attach the 90 degree bend to the large plate using a screw cap in front and fixing it firmly with a wide washer and double nut from behind. Place felt washers between the metal parts and the china surface to prevent it from cracking or grinding through later.

Set the saucer on the end of the "U" curve with a metal plate cap beneath and the cup on top. Separate all parts with felt pads. Thread these together firmly. Screw a bridge socket on to the protruding pipe nipple in the cup. Thread a #18 lamp cord through the curved electrical pipe and screw one end to the binding posts of the lamp socket. Slip the candle collar in place and screw in a small flame lamp. If a lead-in is exposed in the wall, then tie in a short wire to it leading from this newly made lamp. Tape the terminals properly and hang up the plate bracket lamp to hide the lead-in. If no such feed wire is available, attach a wall socket plug to the extension wire, first checking to see that the wire is long enough to reach the nearest outlet.

Use a three wire "finger-grip" which grips the plate rim as a means of hanging this bracket lamp to the wall. There are several such available in the market or at your local hardware, electrical or decorator's shop.

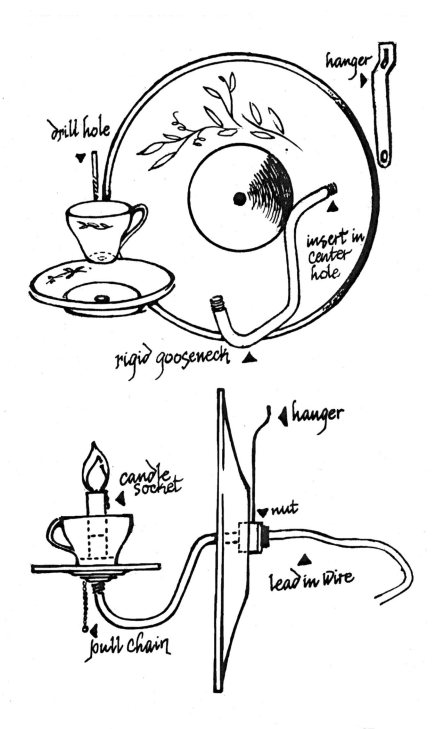

drill hole

hanger

insert in center hole

rigid gooseneck

candle socket

hanger

nut

lead in wire

pull chain

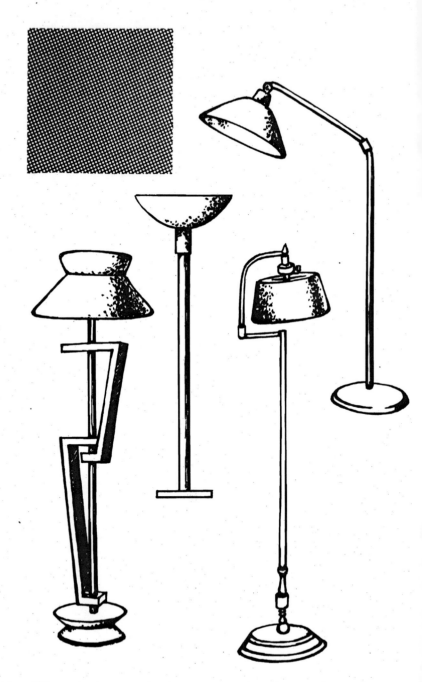

# Portable Floor Lamp

As we consider the portable group—the floor lamp in particular—we should review a few thoughts about the principles of lighting. It is necessary that no glare exist in the room. To permit this is to give eye fatigue, consequently followed by general body tiredness, our official sanction. This is not to be. Glare, therefore, whether directly from the lamp or coming indirectly from some glossy wall or bouncing off a picture glass, is to be carefully avoided. Secondly, since man has developed his ability to live by his sight, he has been accommodating his vision to reflected light from below his eye level and shading or diffusing his original source from overhead. Witness the need of the protective hair-dos of such groups as the Seminole Indians and the head gear developed by farmers, out-of-door workers and soldiers. All of this tends to prove the biologic need for this adjustment. Hence, portable lamps should not be too high, should cast the major portion of their illumination downward and should be shielded from thrusting light directly into the eyes of the person no matter what his position should be in relation to that lamp.

Further eye consideration is that its structure is intended to adjust itself to changing intensities. If we study the out-of-doors where man originally funcioned and developed, we would find that overall changes in light were never radical. It ran the gamut from bright daylight to stygian darkness, but this never happened with any great degree of suddenness. This should show us that general room illumination should not run to extremes in intensity and that changes between rooms or even general areas in the room should not be too strongly opposed in the scale.

Furthermore, at any time during the day or night out-of-doors, the normal difference of illumination between the highlight and the shadow of an area is not extreme. To all this the eye has been developed to make its adjustment. It follows, therefore, that general or key light of a room should not be extreme in either direction. This will bring on early fatigue, whether we wish it or not. Once the proper key light is set, the specific lighting such as supplied by a floor or table lamp must create highlights and shadows but not too far up and down the scale beyond the general illumination of the room. About a thirty per cent variation is adequate— then toward the highlights and about twenty into the shadow area. The eye can stand more of the shadow because it does not excite or stimulate the optic nerve. So, avoid constant general light without shading it to avoid fatigue and create shadows through the correlated highlights to provide resting areas for the observer.

Color is another factor in this review because it's been proved that stimulation can be increased with the use of certain hues, intensities and combinations (juxtapositioning). Likewise restfulness and seditation can be controlled. Selection of color, therefore, must be based upon the kind of room, its size, its function and the specific purpose of a particular area.

# 50 *Lamps and Shades*

### CHAIR-LEG—LAMP with MICA SHADE

Odd pieces of spindle turnings like those of chair and table legs may easily be converted to end-table lamps. Turn an ample base plate to be used under this spindle piece then drill through the center of both. Insert a pipe to hold the parts firmly together and set a lamp socket on top. Embed the bottom holding screw into the base to avoid lamp rocking and table scratching. The body piece may be given a metallic finish, even "antiqued", painted or wood finished if the natural grain permits. In the former case, the lampshade could be covered with metallic cloth and edges bound by tape having metal rings threaded over it.

### WALL-LAMP SCREEN

Bend a length of baling wire to the shape of the frame shown. Form the side panels gently tapering the ends to fit smoothly along the side pieces of the center panel. Solder these firmly together. Thread the extending arms of the screen through clamp-jaw plates made of medium gauge tin-plate. Solder these in place to keep them from twisting. Wrap a sheetmetal clip over these crossed arms. Pinch it close, then secure it firmly with soft solder. Paint it in gay colors. Add ribbed or smooth translucent plastic panels to fill the open areas. Drill holes around the edges by which it may be to the frame with plastic lace.

### SOLID SHADE

Mark off and cut two pieces of $\frac{1}{8}$ cork. Each should fit half-way around a truncated, circular, wire lamp shade frame. Bind the cork covering to the top and bottom shade loops with a like-hued pas partout tape. Where the ends of these cork pieces touch each other, lash them together with wide Florentine leather lace. Cross-thread it through the holes punched in correct position. Spray tempera paint over patterned stencils, cut-outs or template masks to get a bottom border design. Protect the paint, lace, cork and tape with a film of plastic spray. Additional coats may be added if necessary.

### RAW-EDGED PANEL SHADE

Cut four rectangular sides out of $\frac{1}{8}''$ mahogany plywood, each measuring 12 x 9" and the top panel one foot square. Drill a series of holes parallel to the edges of these panels except at the bottom. No holes are drilled there. Twist a double strand of soft thin (28 gauge) copper wire into not too tight a spiral. Anneal the wire to soften it again. Finish the panels in a very high gloss finish before assembling them. Drill a $\frac{1}{4}''$ hole on center of the one-foot panel. Cement a wide $\frac{1}{4}''$ washer to the underside. Lash the panels to each other by threading a spiraling wire through the matching holes with an "over-cast stitch". Twist the ends into a tight roll close to the end hole at the underside of the panels. Spray or brush this copper "lace" with clear lacquer to retain its high polish.

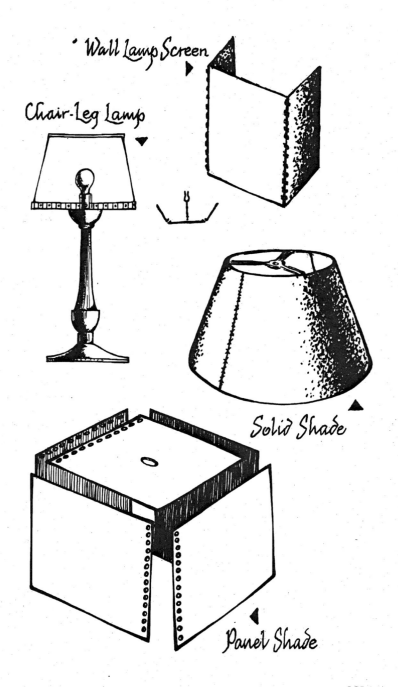

Wall Lamp Screen ▶

Chair-Leg Lamp ▼

Solid Shade ▲

Panel Shade ◀

101

## APRON-DRAPED SHADE

Color and polish a plywood disc of desired size. Attach a soft, fine, wire mesh or a plastic net-weave cloth to its edge as a skirt. Gather the material as close as possible to give it the grace of fullness. Cover the joint with an ornamental tape or plastic molding trim. Bind the lower edge with tape or make a fold-over hem to avoid a raw "finish." Fasten the shade to the lamp harp at its screw post to secure it.

## RIBBED PLASTIC SHIELD

Heat and form a piece of opal, ribbed, thermoplastic material to curve around the front of a pin-up lamp. Smooth the edges before shaping them. Drill holes to accommodate soft rivets which should be fastened to a metal holding plate. This, in turn, is attached to a pinch clamp used to grip the shield piece to the candle socket of the pin-up lamp. This shield may be clamped on and off quickly and easily.

## TOLE CONE

A circular pattern, as shown in the diagram, is cut out of lightweight tinplate and rolled to form a flat cone. Fasten it with a series of flat-beaded rivets in a straight line through the overlapping flap. It may be sweat soldered if preferred. The base lip of the shade may be left raw but smooth, bent back to form a narrow fold or be soldered edge flush to a piece of baling wire. Attach an inner ring and spider near its apex to which a lamp harp can be connected. Paint the lampshade in bright lacquer colors. Pennsylvania Dutch designs are in good taste for this shape of an informal shade. In a more formal vein it might tend toward classical border units like floral, frets or sea inspired motifs.

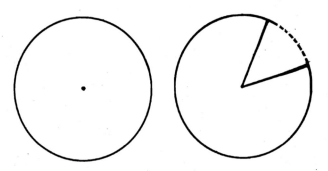

## PAPER-DECOUPAGE SHADE

Trace the pattern shape of a lamp frame on a piece of construction paper and cut it out. Punch a set of evenly-spaced holes along both edges, then set the paper "skin" in position on the frame. Hold it in place with strategically-placed spring clothes pins while it is attaching it to the frame. Bind them together with lace made of crepe paper cut into thin strips and twisted to resemble string. Join the overlapping edges of the paper covering with rubber cement. Do the same with any loose lace ends. Cut out a floral pattern from a selected piece of wallpaper and cement it to the surface of the lamp shade. A protective coating of clear lacquer or plastic spray should keep it safe from injury due to atmospheric changes and hard handling.

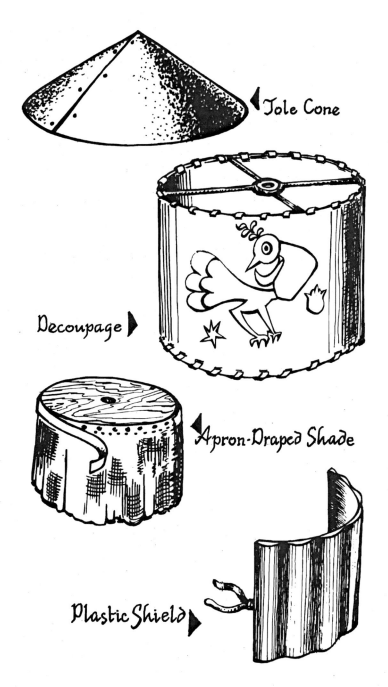

Tole Cone

Decoupage

Apron-Draped Shade

Plastic Shield

## PLASTIC-COATED SCREENING

This lampshade only needs the top wire-loop although the one at the bottom may help keep it firmer. Cut a rectangular strip of plastic dipped, porchwire screening. Roll one long edge over the top wire loop and cement the raw edge around it. Do the same at the bottom. The wire screening is rigid enough to support its own weight and needs no cross-bracing. The fine mesh acts as a diffusing screen to break up the raw light of the lamp light inside even though it is transparent. Color may be added by painting pre-defined areas with any of the aniline dyes available.

## WIRE-LATTICED SHADE

Half inch, square, galvanized chicken wire, cut to sufficient rectangular length should make a sturdy lampshade frame. Cut the wires past the dimension mark just up to the next parallel wire line, leaving a series of wire fingers extending beyond the required size. These are used to wrap around the cross-wire at the edge next to it or around a heavy wire ring serving as a finishing edge. Half inch square, metal clips might be used as an alternative method. A round or rectalinear piece serving as a top plate will help to reinforce it greatly. Weave heavy wool yarn threads in and out of the holes according to a pattern laid out on squared paper. This creates a design on the lampshade resembling a coarse hand-loomed rug.

## FRAMED PANEL SHADE

Flat curtain rods cut lengthwise or brass "U" shaped, single track show case molding can be made into panel frames. This is notched and soldered to proper size and shape. Before each panel is sealed an ornamental glass slide must be inserted. These panels may be fastened to each other and to the spider hoop on top before the glass pieces are set in. This might protect them from heat fracture during the soldering process. The metal frame should be properly smoothed, cleaned and painted before using it as the lampshade.

## ACCORDION PLEATED SHADE

Crease a long strip of thin but tough construction paper in a series of alternate and parallel folds. The raw edges may be doubled back and pasted down or straddled with half inch wide pas partout tape, for reinforcement. Punch matching and aligned holes through the vertical center of each folded panel and about two inches from each end. Thread a decorative braid or cord through each set of these holes. By drawing them tightly or not the diameter size of the shade at that point may be regulated to suit the spider hoop which it covers. In that way the general form of the shade can be controlled. Fasten it to the supporting wire rings with tape or lash string.

## SWIVEL-LOUVRED SHADE

This lampshade is made of a series of parallel plastic fins. One side of each one is wrapped around a thick aluminum wire and cemented. These louvres are held in place by two, one-half-inch rings of 10 gauge aluminum. One is on top, the other at the bottom of these end-pivoting pieces. The wire pins extending out of each end of these rings are inserted into matched holes drilled through these aluminum rings. Two long wires are anchored in special holes in the bottom ring, extend up vertically through aligned holes in the top ring, bends at right angles across the top of the shade and return on the diametrically opposite side in reverse order. The spider wires cross at right angles on center on top and form a flat loop. This is used to attach the lampshade to the harp.

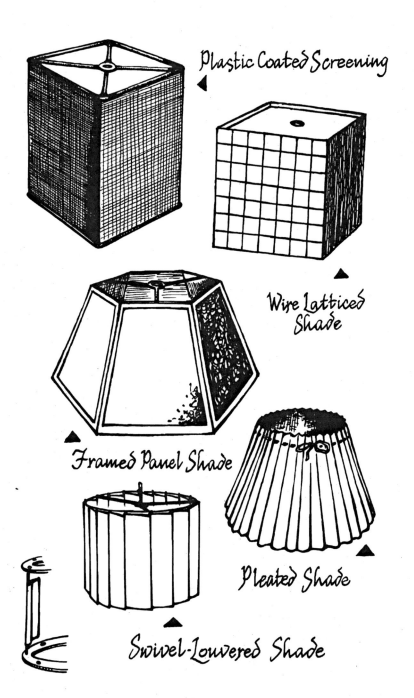

Plastic Coated Screening ◄

Wire Latticed Shade ▲

Framed Panel Shade ▲

Pleated Shade ▲

Swivel-Louvered Shade ▲

## RAFFIA-WRAPPED SHADE

Raffia, any other yarn-like material should serve as well, may be wrapped around the wire "arms" of the lamp shade frame in many arrangements to result in a variety of designs. In wrapping the raffia material, it will have to be joined at the ends to lengthen it for continued use. When completed, some kind of protective coating should be used to cover this highly vulnerable material—vulnerable to dirt, moisture and destruction.

## BAMBOO SPLINT SHADE

A series of bamboo splint, drilled at both ends are lashed to top and bottom rims of a lampshade frame with plastic tie string or fishing line. Set the splints parallel to each other and overlapping slightly. This shields the light more effectively. The natural finish of bamboo is highly desirable though it may be stained or dip-dyed to match the color scheme of the room.

## LATTICED-TOP SHINGLE SHADE

Two sets of long one inch wide strips of flexible plastic material (.050 thick) are set crossing each other in units of 8, 10, or 12 depending upon the desired size of the shape. A square is fashioned in basket-weave ending by wrapping around the top of the wire frame of a square lampshade. The ends are cemented down firmly. Starting at the bottom of the shade wind rows over row of the same strips so that the one above overlaps the strip directly below it for about an eighth of an inch. These wrappings are individual rings whose ends are firmly cemented at one of the corners. The entire construction resembles the siding of a frame house.

## NEON BOUDOIR LAMP

The base of this lamp contains the rectifying mechanism needed for neon wiring. The light switch is connected at that point. The neon tubing travels up the pedestal of large ribbed glass tube in which it will glow and cause the lampstand to be illuminated. Of the two extending neon lead tubes, one will travel straight up, bend out at right angles then curl down in an increasing spiral following the walls of an imaginary drum-shaped lampshade. The bottom end of this connects with the other lead tube, making a complete circuit. A hood of the same shape and made of either very finely meshed aluminum wire screening or of flexible plastic sheeting, plain or figured, is set over it to help diffuse the raw quality of this light. This lamp has a low efficiency point.

## PLASTIC-CARVED FLUORESCENT LAMP

Cut two, one-inch pieces of Lucite to the indicated shape and polish all surfaces except the edges. Carve an intaglio design on the inside surface of the front section. Use a hand-grinder in much the same manner as a dentist would. Clamp the two halves together with the gray-carved design between them. Set "U" shaped aluminum channels over each edge of these joined pieces of plastic and fasten them with plastic drive screws. Fit the ballast and switch into the hollowed base section, threading the lead wire up one aluminum channel. A short fluorescent lamp is fixed to the top of this Lucite lamp back. Fashion an aluminum shade having two tool clips riveted to the inside of it. These will snap on to the fluorescent tube to shield the eyes from direct light and support the shade. The entire lamp will glow when lit up.

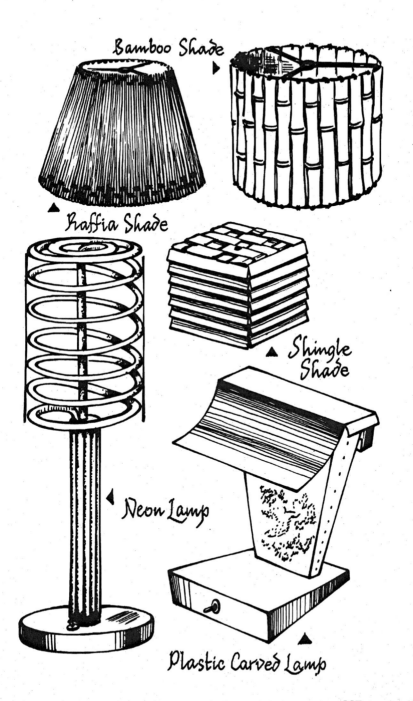

Bamboo Shade

Raffia Shade

Shingle Shade

Neon Lamp

Plastic Carved Lamp

## FLEXIBLE, INDIRECT SPOT—TABLE REFLECTOR

A short parabolic reflector bowl is fastened to a hard spring flexible gooseneck. The base is a domed fixture cap mounted on a large weighted automobile hub cap. This is connected to the gooseneck. A ring made of half-inch "L" beam is riveted to three rigid wire legs ending in a socket collar clamp. The ring is drilled and tapped for thumb control set-screws to hold an encased Fresne lens. If the metal is match it may be buffed to a high gloss. If not, paint it with a contrasting crackle paint over an undercoat of colored lacquer. Wire it with a base switch. The lamp serves as an indirect light and for special needs as a spot light.

## CANOPY PEDESTAL LAMP

A serrated glass tube of reasonable diameter is mounted on a small, inverted cut-glass bowl or square sided dish with a hole drilled through its center. Hold these together with a length of electrical pipe and capped at each end, properly protected against breakage. Attach a one-lamp socket and harp on top and wire it for incandescent lighting. Make the "canopy shade" of any of the many transparent casting resins. Follow, very carefully, the directions given with the plastic compound. Use an appropriately-shaped glass mixing bowl or metal wash basin. After it has been cured drill for the harp screw and anchor it with a glass finial. These, glass and plastic, may be made of tinted material.

## MODERN VANITY LAMP

Screw a one and a half inch square, polished brass tubing into the notched corner of a two inch thick polished walnut base about eight inches square. Braze four wire prong supports for the ring which hangs over the lamp. Wire it with a pull chain socket after setting in a walnut plug-cap with a pipe nipple through it to hold the socket in place. Make the shade of walnut veneer cemented on a linen back (U. S. Plywood Corp.). Glue the flap-over edge to make a clean cut joint. Make a grooved reflector-rest attachment to dip low and rest on the lamp ring previously made. Use a thin, soft brass strip to edge the lamp and flap over the top and bottom lampshade rings to help lampshade keep its shape and remain firm.

## DRIFTWOOD LAMP

A well-chosen, weather-worn piece of driftwood log can make a very interesting time-sculptured pedestal for a lamp. Drill a hole through its vertical center large enough to accommodate a section of threaded pipe. Have it extend through the base piece (also driftwood) and extend up sufficiently to set a push button socket. A round tapered shade covered with natural colored Monk's cloth should look well with the darker toned driftwood. The lamp body and base may be highlighted with ochre or buff to contrast with the deep brown tones of the crevices. A section of driftwood branch will make a proper looking finial. Wire it and you have a fine ranch house or modern-looking lighting piece.

## NEWEL-POST—PEDESTAL LAMP

Bannister newel posts have been turned in many interesting forms and a section of a discarded one can be converted into an unusual pedestal lamp. Saw off as much of the top section as would look well and drill down through its center to accommodate a section of electrical pipe. Extend it and add the necessary fixture to hold an opal glass reflector bowl. Set a silk-covered, wire framed lampshade on it to rest upon the bowl's edge. Attach a base plate large enough to give it sufficient stability, then wire it for incandescent lighting. The silk shade might have another colored lining to create color interest when the lamp is lit.

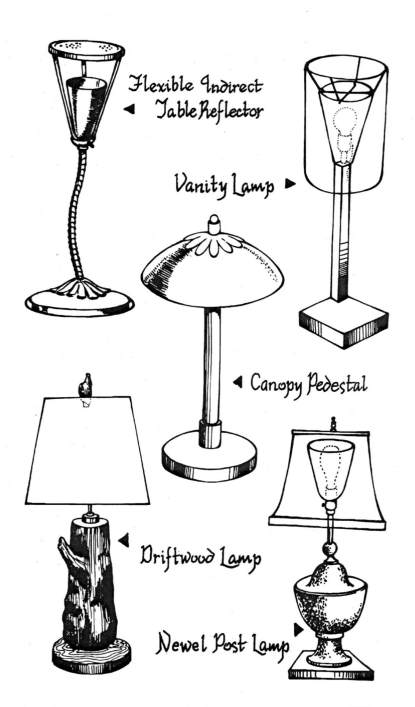

Flexible Indirect
◄ Table Reflector

Vanity Lamp ►

◄ Canopy Pedestal

◄ Driftwood Lamp

Newel Post Lamp ►

## BAMBOO LAMP—METAL SHADE

This lamp seeks its realization through the use of lengths of bamboo shoots. A sturdy-sized section should serve as the pedestal piece with a wood plug in each end holding the electrical pipe in position. Greater width for base-stability may be added by lashing to the bottom section with shorter pieces of bamboo with split reeds. These too, may be plugged and so serve as a planter lamp in addition. A bottom piece of wood may be cut to matching silhouette to cap the individual bamboo vessels as one. Wire the lamp with either single socket and harp or a double socket attachment. The lamp shade is cut and fashioned out of a section of fancy radiator metal grill, bordered along the top and bottom rims with template—silhouette strips soldered to it. Polish or lacquer it as desired. Use a small bamboo section as a finial piece.

## WROUGHT-IRON—LYRE LAMP

This is an excellent porch lamp though it can be used for other parts of the house, if suitable in style. The body is made of 1 x 2 inch rectangular tubing. The harp form is shaped of 1″ x ¼″ strap iron. The "strings" are ¼″ rods. The bottom of the strap iron harp is punched through (heated first) and forged open to permit the center tube to ease through it. The string rods are inserted into holes and mushroomed at the ends to hold firmly in place. The upper ends are fastened together by two strips of 1/16-inch sheet metal with rivets spaced to do the job. A cap set on the top of the tube serves to hold a threaded electrical pipe which connects to the dual-socket unit. The bottom place through a hole in the rectangular, chamfered marble base, splayed open then cemented. The shade is shaped in front and back with sides as fill-in panels. This wire frame with a molding grill on top and solid strip on bottom is covered with spun glass. Paint all metal parts.

## ROPE-TWIST—WOOD LAMP

Carve or turn a twenty-two inch length by three inches in diameter wooden rope twist. Finish in dark wood color. Cut out a ten inch heavy wooden disc for the base. Finish that in natural light color. Attach a strip of light colored, linen-backed wood veneer (matching the bases) around a ten-inch drum wire lampshade frame. Attach it with dark ¼ inch wide rawhide lace with an overcast stitch. Drill or punch holes in the veneer to accommodate the lace. Before assembling the lamp, cut off a two inch section to serve as a finial. Top it with a 1½ inch wooden ball. Screw the base to the pedestal rope, drill for and insert the lamp cord. Use a threaded nipple on top to attach the lamp socket and the harp to the rope. Arrange to have the lead-in wire emerge from the side of the base block. Cement a felt pad under it for scratch-protection.

## DECANTER LAMP

A large, Italian wine bottle half covered with reed and raffia dressing is the basis of an interesting novelty lamp. Drill a hole in its bottom and set in a piece of electrical pipe to extend about four inches above its lip. Slide a cork bushing into the bottle mouth to hold the pipe securely upright. Wrap multicolored strips of raffia in continuous vertical windings around a wire lampshade frame. Pack these strands close together allowing no flapping or sagging of each wrapping. Spray a plastic coat or brush it lightly with a thinned solution of white shellac to help protect the shade. Convert one of the Swiss novelty wood-carved corks into a lamp finial to top it off. If the lamp appears top heavy, fill the bottle with beach sand. This will add greater stability. Select a bottle having colored glass, if possible.

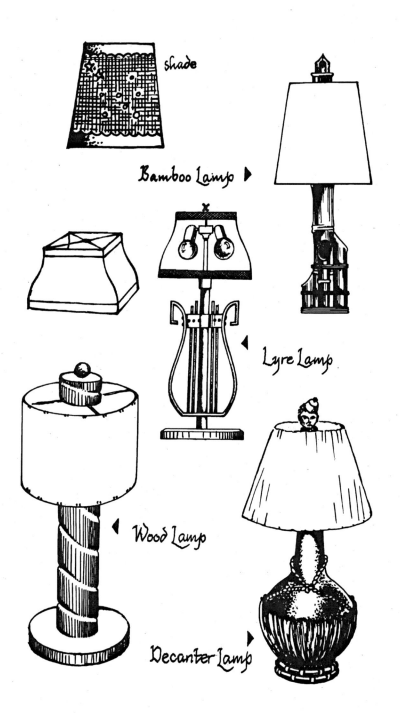

shade

Bamboo Lamp ▶

Lyre Lamp

Wood Lamp ◀

Decanter Lamp ▶

## GLASS BRICK—UTILITY LAMP

Make this lamp starting with a large glass brick. Drill holes through the center, top and bottom to accommodate the pipe necessary for wiring. This pipe should be long enough to pass through the wood block base, the glass brick and a metal or wooden cap plate. It is gripped at the bottom with a lock nut set in a counter-bored hole and on top with coupling nut to permit the addition of the lamp socket section. The lampshade is made of four tapered panels of eighth inch plywood. Decorate each with a pierced design. Join them at the corners with angle irons set inside and fastened with split rivets. The finial which repeats the material of the body of the lamp is made of clear plastics with scored cross lines to simulate the effect of the glass brick. Thread the bottom hole directly or use a screw insert.

## CHILD'S PIN-UP LAMP

Several large children's play blocks are used for the body of this lamp. Drill a set of half-inch aligned holes through them. In the center block drill one at right angles to it. Counterbore half way in on the original hole to accommodate an outside pipe barrel bushing with a right angle threaded hole. Link all these together with short threaded pipe sections. Use flange plates on the outside to clamp these blocks together. Use a short extension nipple to set the lamp off the correct distance from the wall plate which is a painted plywood cut-out. Add the lamp socket section to the top. Convert a toy drum of the right size to become the shade. Remove one side and insert the wired washer so that it sets firmly upon the harp screw.

## LIBRARY—TABLE LAMP

This lamp is purely an assembly job. All parts are stock pieces available at most every metal drawing and spinning parts company. The size and complication of the lamp depends upon the ability of the craftsman to conceive a unit. The lampshade is built upon a wire frame. The "lamp skin" is cut and mounted. Binding tape is an effective material and does an excellent job in holding the stretched parchment to the lampshade hoops. Cut-out pieces of stained mica are cemented along the top edge. Nail heads decoration gives a wide latitude to an imaginative decoration.

## SPIRAL SHIELD—ADJUSTABLE LAMP

The vertical upright pipe, screwed into a heavy, metal base much like that which supports merchandise display stands, becomes the stanchion for the bridge arm. This arm is clamped over the upright allowing it to be moved up or down and fixed at any given position. The lamp socket section is attached to the end of the extending arm with a swivel joint. The shield is made of a pennant-shaped triangular piece of frosted lumarith. This is anchored along the top edge of the plastic to the socket holder causing the spiral and progressive reduction of the size of the shield toward the inside of it.

## ADJUSTABLE DESK LAMP

Two 1" x ½" oval brass pipe posts, topped by a square brass cross pipe bar serve as the supports for this adjustable lamp. Four inch long slots by ¼" wide are cut just below the top of these posts to accommodate the threaded nipple and thumb screw catch which supports the "S" curved metal shade. The front end of the nipple ends at a right angle elbow connecting to a keyless lamp socket which holds a long lumiline lamp. The connecting wire leads down the oval post into the underside of the gaily colored wooden base to be connected to the canopy push switch.

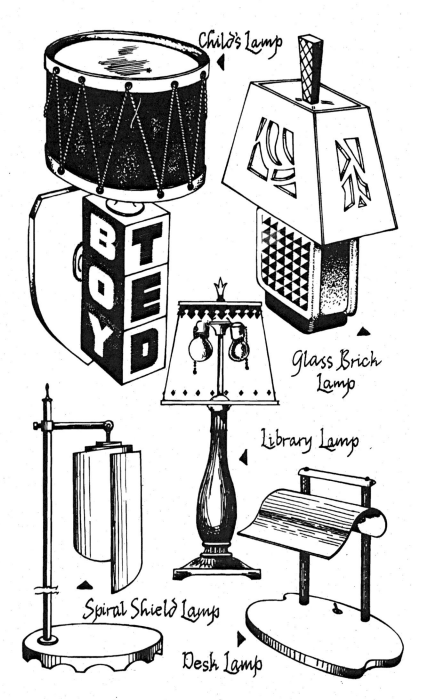

Child's Lamp

Glass Brick Lamp

Library Lamp

Spiral Shield Lamp

Desk Lamp

## "CHUCKLE-WOOD" LAMP

This "chuckle-wood" material, produced by the U. S. Plywood Corp., is cut into square mounds resembling small pyramids and mounted on a cloth backing. A section of this is cut to make up the proper height and when curled, the correct-sized cylinder. Glue the matching edges from the inside with a tape against the cloth side of the material. Cap each end with a block of wood and clamp the whole thing tightly with a piece of electrical pipe, washer and screw at each end. See that the pipe extends about four inches above to which the lamp socket and harp are screwed. Finish this in any of the popular wood finishes. A simple drum-shaped shade covered with opaque plastic film will look good. A checkered square border design cemented to it along the rim will carry out a repeat of the squared motif of the lamp base itself.

## UPHOLSTERED LEATHER LAMP

Around a hollow wooden plinth of a lamp base tack down a padded leather cover with upholsterer's button nails to form an all-over diamond pattern. Finish off the top and bottom by rolling under the raw leather edges and fastening it down in a continued pattern of the button-padded design. The exposed sections of the wood are painted before being upholstered. Natural colored leather with matching buttons against a contrasting-hued paint should go well with a buff-colored lampshade made of coarse-weave, wooly-fibered knubby cloth. The finial is the inverted shape of the base painted to match the leather tones and dotted in diaper design. Use an antiqued brass nail whose head-shape resembles the puffed area of the upholstery created by button identations.

## TUBE TWISTED—ROPE LAMP

Three lengths of half or five-eighths inch aluminum or brass tubing (whichever suits the group decoration) are spirally twisted over a tapered sleeve. These are welded to a base plate and cap as shown. Through one of these the lamp cord is drawn starting from a hole in the base plate which opens into the tube and out of a hole in the side of the tube just below the top cap. This, then leads into a pipe nipple screwed into the center hole of the cap ending in the lamp socket within the reflector globe. The lamp shades rests; hangs on the globe edges by its formed wires. Its upper trim is enhanced by the repetition of the round wire open spiral which carries on the motif of the lamp base.

## WASH DAY, PIN-UP LAMP

This doll lamp has a half silhouetted wooden and painted figure with pinned arms, one of which pivots and when it does, pulls the lamp's chain switch. The shade is made of bamboo splints lashed to a half wash basket shape and clipped on to the lamp bulb for attachment. The wiring follows through a piece of electrical pipe which is strap-anchored into a half-round dado groove cut along the back spine of the figure. This bends forward on top in a short "S" curve ending with the lamp socket. This enables the lamp bulb to be centered within the shade. Screw a bracket plate on the back and as close to the top of the body as possible to keep it from spinning head downward when hung against the wall.

## BEAN POLE ADJUSTABLE FLOOR LAMP

Use a five foot length of polished, square metal tubing for the bean pole body of this floor lamp. Seal the top with a snap-on plate cap and attach the bottom to a galleried, platter-like base piece by brazing it. The lamp shade, a truncated square pyramid is made of coarse cotton shantung

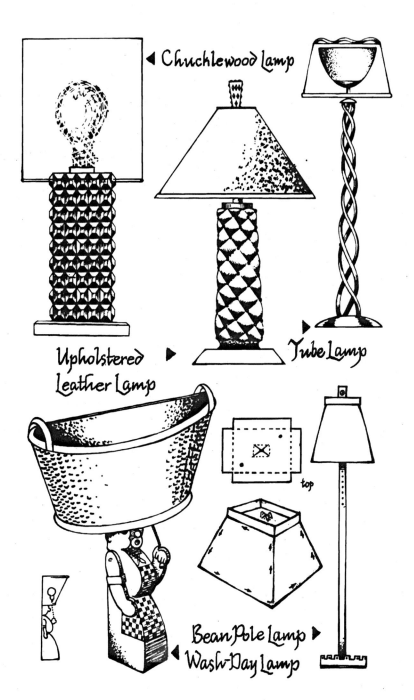

◀ Chucklewood Lamp

Upholstered Leather Lamp ▶

▶ Tube Lamp

top

Bean Pole Lamp ▶

◀ Wash-Day Lamp

material with a large-figured, block-printed lining. This will create a highly decorated lampshade every time the lights are switched on in the lamp and an unadorned one when the lights go off. The lamps themselves are wired to the structure of the shade so that they move with the adjustment of the shade. This holds firmly to the pole by the spring action of the dimples in the flanges matching those made in the pole. The lamp cord extends through the pole and is spring-curled like telephone extensions to open and contract as used.

## WROUGHT-IRON BIRD CAGE FLOOR LAMP

A "barrel bird cage" made of three heavy wire hoops and joined by four vertical support rods are, in turn, welded to a $5/8''$ lamp pipe rack. This is bent into a large circular base to create sufficient stability. The hoops of the "bird cage" may serve as a support for shelves made of heavy gauge, close-meshed screen. The upper end of the pipe rack terminates with the lamp socket and harp on which a wicker-woven, reed shade is supported. The lamp cord extends down through the lamp rack and emerges from an opening at some point of the ring base.

## BOWLING GLOBE LAMP

Convert a large bowling or duck pin into a lamp by drilling a hole through its center from top through the bottom. Screw a wooden base plate to it and set in an electrical pipe to hold the lamp cord safely. Attach the lamp socket at the top and a round globe holder to it. Select one which most resembles the size of a bowling ball. If an opaque or heavy translucent glass is unavailable then coat the inside of the globe with oil paint of the chosen color. Get a uniform covering without brush streaks showing by patting the half-wet paint with a cheesecloth pounce ball. Use a pull chain socket switch for convenience.

## PLANTER'S LAMP

Secure a fair sized hammered copper flower pot and flat bowl to match. Drill a hole in the bottom of the pot and bolt a brass pipe, threaded on both ends, with a lock nut and washer on each side of the hole. Brace the pipe at the lip-level of the pot with two brass cross wires (11 gauge) which circle the pipe, then are riveted securely in holes at opposite sides of the pot lip. These four braces should be ample. Solder the pot, on center, to the flat bowl with a flat "Z" or "C" foot to raise it about one inch above the bowl bottom. Shape and solder some lengths of galvanized baling wire to form a trellis with two long pricking prongs at its bottom. Paint it to suit. The lampshade is the wire structure covered with colored translucent lumarith. The top hoop has a copper wire wave shaped and soldered to it. Use an exposed copper wire at the bottom too. Wire it, set your plant in order then fill the bowl with an assortment of colored glass marbles.

## COLONIAL BRACKET LAMP

A piece of thin stock wrought iron wall plate is forged to the shape shown. Two lips are cut, drilled and bent out to serve as the swivel prongs for the bracket arm. Form the vertical plate for the bracket and join the horizontal and the twisted bracing arm to it. Use a long iron rivet pin to connect the arms with its vertical plate and to the swivel prongs. The front end of the bracket is forged flat and both pieces drilled together to accept a short nipple. Make an open harp whose three arms open on top to allow a lampshade to rest solidly on its forked prongs. Add a candle socket with the thumb twist switch extending below. The lamp shade, made

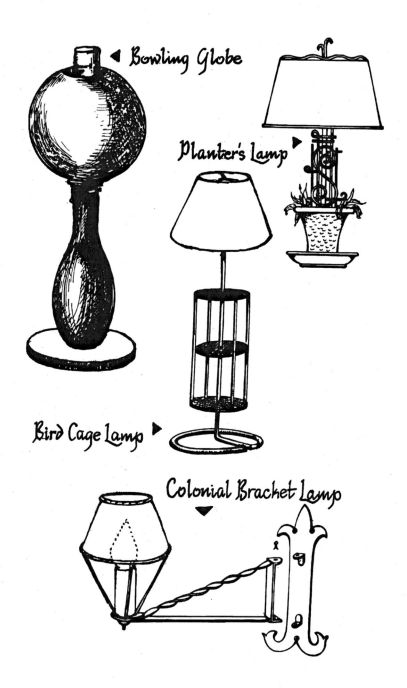

◀ Bowling Globe

Planter's Lamp ▶

Bird Cage Lamp ▶

Colonial Bracket Lamp
▼

of antiqued paper parchment has two heavy metal hoops framing it. The lamp cord is carried back along the bracket arm to accommodate itself to the swing.

## TELESCOPING DESK LAMP

This lamp requires a wide, weighted base to maintain its stability no matter how the lamp is maneuvered. A long metal hood, somewhat resembling a section of roofing gutter is closed at both ends and attached to a flange arm on its center. Set in a single light 20 watt fluorescent unit with its push-button switch at the top, center of the lighthood. A long piece of frosted plastics with half-inch strips cemented inside in parallel rows to act as louvres is clip-hinged to the front edge of the reflector hood. These hinges should be tight so that they remain in position even if only partially open. A fifteen inch square tube is fastened to the base and joined at the top to a telescoping arm by a universal swivel joint. The telescoping extension resembles that type of collapsible camera tripod leg excepting that each section is no more than eight inches. The thin end uses an elbow joint to connect with the lamp unit of the structure. This may be made in polished metal or painted to suit the room harmony. The lamp base may be of marble or weighted wood.

## COLONIAL BRACKET CLAMP-ON

This lamp is intended as an auxiliary piece to be clamped on to some end or occasional table. The upright is a wooden square along which the sliding bracket mechanism moves. The weight of the extension arm and lampshade throws the vertical alignment of the sliding arm off causing it to thrust inward and pinch clamp itself to the pole. The upper gripping arm simply slides down holding the bracket arm pin in place to permit it to swing. The fastening device on the bottom works in much the same way excepting that the side thrust is caused by the pressure exerted by the wooden thumb screw. A long nipple and swivel joint holds the lamp socket in place. The lamp shade grips the socket by its uno-bridge fitting. Cretonne or chintz makes an excellent combination with cherry or maple.

## MOBILE—CANDELABRA

A metal, square tapered shank set upon an inverted metal plate is a fine body for this candelabra. This upper part of the shank is topped with a dual-socket attachment into each of which a fifteen inch polished, flexcable, gooseneck is attached. On the free end of the gooseneck a cubed box is set. The extension arm enters one side, the thumb-turn switch extends from the bottom and a cup and candle socket is attached. The individual-sized lamp shade fits above the candle sleeve with a uno-bridge attachment fixed to the bottom hoop of the shade. All this enables one to bend the arms to many and varied positions either symmetrically or in occultly asymmetric balance lending it a modern touch.

## VANITY—CLUSTER LAMP

Attach two, shaped and rigid pipes to bottom of deep, metal and weighted bowl. Add a length of flexible gooseneck shaft to each with an outside coupling or bushing. The free end is connected to a metal bowl reflector with an oval harp under the lamp socket. Set a metal reflector plate on the harp screw, held down by a button finial. Fix a push button switch in the center of the base bowl, the lamp extension cord exiting from its side. Spray it with a soft-hued crackle color unless it must fit a specific decorative scheme. This lamp has the versatility of acting as a candelabrum, as a pair of lamps or as individual units serving different, though close-by areas.

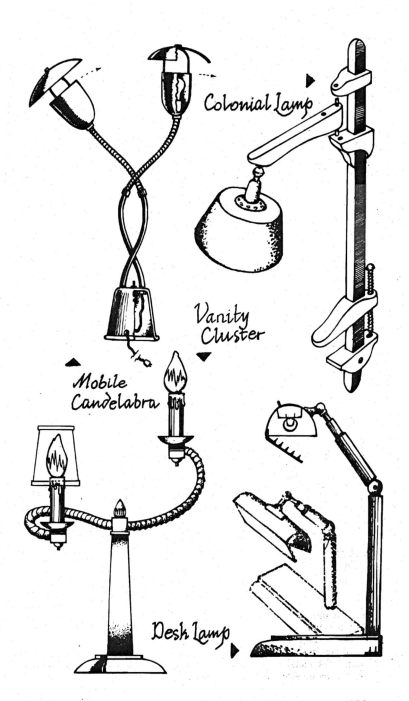

Colonial Lamp

Vanity Cluster

Mobile Candelabra

Desk Lamp

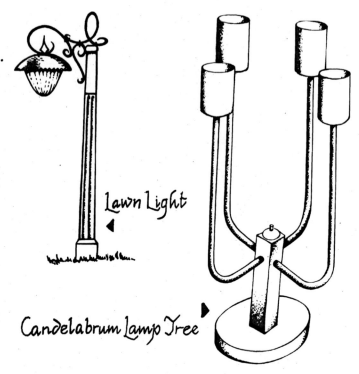

*Lawn Light* ◀

*Candelabrum Lamp Tree* ▶

## LAWN LIGHT

This is a private street lamp which has a wooden post built around the B-X cable which comes out of its ground outlet box extending up to the lamp at the top. The post may be reeded, fluted, or kept unadorned except for its base and cap piece. The wrought iron pieces should be shaped out of shallow "U" bar except where the B-X cable extends toward the lamp socket. There deeper "U" bars or even hollow square iron tubes might be used to hide the ungainly cable. The metal reflector shade acts as a weather protecting canopy for the socket section. The bottom glass globe is so fastened that it may be removed as needed without too much complication. Protect all exposed parts with outdoor paint to match the color scheme of its surroundings.

## CANDELABRUM LAMP TREE

Four deep drum shades made of spun glass on wire frames clip on to the individual lamp bulbs of this candelabrum. The sockets tip four very long, vertical pipe arms which bend in on short, graceful 90° curves to be fastened to a center, metal tubular post. This, in turn, is brazed on to a large diametered circular disc with vertical sides. The top of this hollow post terminates with a cap in which a decorative push button switch is inserted. The length of the post and arms are optional and determined by the place in decoration it will occupy as is the wattage and size of the lamps. The metal frame may be of polished metal like brass, or aluminum or of conglomerate metals which are finally painted.

# Conclusion

## Glossary of Terms

**A.C. CURRENT**—An electrical charge which alternates its direction of flow at regular intervals.

**ACETATE**—General name for fabric made from cellulose acetate yarns such as Celanese, Acele, Seraceta, Rayon.

**ACRYLATE RESIN**—One of the group of acrylic resins in the glasslike thermoplasts like Lucite or Plexiglas.

**AMINO PLASTIC**—A synthetic resin (thermoset) made from the amino or amido compounds.

**AMPERE**—Is the measure of how many units (coulombs) of electricity that pass a given point within one second.

**ANODIZING**—A method of coloring and coating a metal with a protective film by subjecting it to an electrolytic action as the anodes of a cell.

**APPLIQUE**—Cut-out ornamentation applied or laid on another. The method of adherence depends upon the materials involved.

**ARTIFICIAL LEATHER**—Substitute for leather. Made of cotton cloth with plastic coating. Embossed and colored to imitate various leathers.

**ASBESTOS**—A fireproof and acid proof material of mineral origin. Long, straight, lustrous fibers spun and woven with cotton; later burned away. Difficult to spin; not dyed.

**BAFFLES**—A series of plates or screens set to cover a lamplight in order to deflect or regulate the light.

**BALANCE**—The state of equilibrium and counterforces achieved by the distribution of visual artistic elements.

**BALLAST**—A current-steadying device used with a fluorescent lamp.

**BASKET CLOTH (Monk's cloth)**—Is a plain-woven fabric with two or more warp threads used as a unit in its weaving.

**BAS-RELIEF (Low Relief)**—The projection of figures and ornamentation from the background to a degree lower than normal.

**BATIK**—Is a Javanese process of resist dyeing on cotton by painting or pouring molten wax in a design to keep it from being colored when the cloth is dip-dyed. The wax is removed afterward. This is imitated by machine printing.

**BATTERY**—A container of a limited reservoir of electrical charge.

**BISCUIT FIRING**—Is first heating of the clay adheres to the ceramic ware.

**BLACK LIGHT**—The light of the ultra-violet scale used to excite fluorescent or phosphorescent materials.

**BLIND TOOLING**—To shape, form or finish ornamentation on leather, etc., without use of gilding, inking or coloring.

**BLOCK PRINTING**—Is the decoration of fabrics by hand printing with carved wooden (sometimes linoleum, cork or rubber) blocks as distinguished from the modern printing with copper rollers.

**BODY**—A term used to designate center portion of a lighting fixture to which the arms and branches are attached.

**BOOK CLOTH**—Is a coarse plain-woven cloth heavily sized and embossed. Its very smooth surface makes easy application of painted or printed decoration.

**BRAZING**—To solder with a relatively infusible alloy such as brass or hard solder.

**BRUSHES**—Are parts of a motor which convey the voltage of a generator out of an outside line or into a motor from an outside source.

**BULB**—Is the bowl, usually glass, which encases the mechanism of the lamp.

**CALENDERING**—Adding a luster and smoothness to linen by passing it through steam rollers.

**CANDLE**—The paper cylinder sleeve which slips over the socket to simulate a candle.

**CELLOPHANE**—Is transparent sheeting of spent cellulose acetate which may be-gotten in an array of colors.

**CERAMICS**—Is the art of making pottery.

**CHASING**—The method of ornamenting by grooving or indenting metal with an embossed or sculptured effect.

**CHINA**—Is a ceramic product which is non-porous, glazed and translucent.

**CHINTZ**—Originally referred to any printed cotton fabric, same as calico did, now is a small gay figured (sometimes large motif) fabric. Some chintzes have a glazed surface and are called "glazed chintz."

**CELLULOSE RESINS**—A group of synthetic thermoplastic materials containing cellulose as its basic chemical.

**CIRCUIT**—Is the path of flow taken by electrical current from its source to its piece of apparatus and back.

COATED FABRIC—A covering or lamination of smooth material on a fabric to give it luster, strength and new texture.

COLD LIGHT—Illumination which is accompanied by low heat, usually free of fluorescent light.

COLORFAST—Is the name applied to certain cotton fabrics whose color will not run when wetted or washed.

COMBINATION CIRCUIT—Is one in which there is both a parallel and a series circuit.

COMPOSITION—Is a substitute for wood, usually pressed in a mold to imitate carvings.

CONDUCTORS—Are those materials which offer little or no resistance to the flow of current.

CONFIGURED GLASS—A patterned or irregular surfacing of glass usually applied during its manufacture. It is not transparent and somewhat diffusing.

CORDUROY—Is derived from the French "corde du Roi" meaning King's cord, is a kind of cotton velvet having ridges or cords in the pile.

COULOMB—Is a unit which measures a definite quantity of electricity that passes a given point within one second.

COVE LIGHT—Illumination which originates in a trench-like strip and usually offers up indirect lighting to the area.

CRASH—Is the term applied to several rough fabrics having coarse uneven yarns and rough textures like crash linen or cotton.

CRAZING—Describes the condition of the surface which has cracked because of uneven cooling and shrinking.

CREPE—Is the general term covering many kinds of crinkled, puckering or unevened surface materials. There are many such effects such as rough, crinkle, flat or plissé crepes.

CRETONNE—Is a printed fabric of cotton or linen in all varieties of weaves and finishes, even chintz.

CRYSTAL—Short for rock-crystal, is a clear variety of quartz which looks like glass but is much harder.

CUT GLASS—Glass, usually flint, which is shaped or ornamented by cutting, grinding and polishing.

CURRENT—Of electricity is the measure (in amperes) of the quantity passing through a conductor in ONE SECOND.

DAMASCENING—The art of decorating metals by forging one metal into the hollowed areas of another metal in imitation of the steel decorating done in early Damascus.

D.C. CURRENT—An electrical charge which flows in one direction only.

DECALCOMANIA—Is a processed paper from which a design may be transferred to another surface.

DECORATED GLASS—A glass to whose surface some manner of decoration is applied.

DECOUPAGE—Paste-on of picture cut-outs upon objects to simulate an effect of inlay or marquetry work.

DIAPER DESIGN—A regular, all-over repeat of a diamond-shaped, trellised pattern.

DIMMER—Is a device used to regulate the flow of electricity distribution systems. It is usually used to reduce or increase the efficiency of the lamp or apparatus not beyond one hundred per cent.

DIRECT LIGHT—Light which reaches its obective directly from its source of illumination.

DIRECT PRINTING—Is the method of printing cloth from engraved rolls or blocks much in the same way wallpaper is printed.

DISCHARGE PRINTING—Is the method of printing on dark materials after the fabric is piece-dyed. The color is removed or bleached from prescribed areas by chemicals to form light-toned units; sometimes called "extract" printing.

DOMINANCE—Achieving controlling attention within a unified group of compositional parts.

DRY CELL BATTERY—A voltaic (electric) cell whose contents has been treated by use of some absorbent carrier to insure its not spilling.

DRYPOINT—A method of engraving with a needle instead of a burin or with acid.

DYEING—Is the process of coloring materials. Variations of this are cross-dyeing, dip-dyeing, ingrain-dyeing, piece-dyeing, stock dyeing or yarn-dyeing.

DYNAMO—Is a term used to include both a motor and a generator. It may be used as either depending upon whether it is being fed mechanical or electrical power. It will deliver the opposite type of energy.

EFFICIENCY—Is the percentage of power delivered by a machine against the power used to supply this same machine. It can never equal 100, it is always less.

ELECTRICITY—Is the flow of current along a conductor.

ELECTROLYTE—A substance in which the conduction of electricity is accomplished by chemical decomposition.

ELECTRODE—Either terminal by which an electric current enters or leaves an electric body source (electrolyte).

EMBOSSING—Is the texture of raised effect gotten by pressing the fabric or leather between engraved rollers with the aid of heat.

ENAMELING—Applying a vitreous composition for coating the surface of metal.

ENERGY and WORK—Is the mechanical energy measured in terms of horsepower X the hours in which it is used.

ENGRAVING—An incising method of producing decorations on wood, metal, stone, etc.

ETCHING—The art of producing designs by means of "biting" into metal with an acid.

EXTENSION CORD—A length of electric wire needed to reach a nearby outlet often used on a portable item.

FABRIC—Is cloth, goods or textile material woven or knitted of any textile fibers.

FELT—Cloth formed by the action of heat, moisture, and friction on wool fibers.

FILAMENT—Is a single strand of fiber or metal used in weaving or as an electric conductor-resistor to bring on incandescence.

FILTERS—A special screen used to partially absorb or change the character of light rays.

FINIAL—The terminal knob or ornament usually the nut which fastens the shade washer to the harp screw or the lowest ornament of the chandelier types.

FINISHING—Refers to all processes after the construction or assemblage process have been completed.

**FLOCKING**—Is the process of applying designs or covering on materials by blowing on ground flocks (fibers of wool, spun glass, asbestos or other fibers) over a surface previously printed, sprayed or painted with an adherent.

**FLUORESCENT**—A type of illumination which depends upon a substance which when stimulated gives off light.

**FLUTING**—Is the decoration achieved by means of parallel channels or flutes.

**FLUX**—A material used in soldering to prevent the metals from oxidizing during the heating process.

**FREQUENCY OF CURRENT**—The number of alternations or directional changes of the A.C. current per second.

**FRET**—Is the ornamental work of an interlaced design, either pierced or a solid background.

**FROSTED GLASS**—A glass whose surface, one or both, have been roughened to increase the diffusion of the light.

**FUR**—Is the hair-covered skin of an animal.

**FUR FABRICS**—Are the large class of pile fabrics which are made to imitate fur.

**FUSE**—Is a protective device in an electric circuit, usually a conductor which melts, thus breaking the circuit at a preset danger point.

**GAUGE**—A measure of thickness standards within specified limits and usually applied to metals and wires.

**GENERAL LIGHT**—Light designed to cover the entire area with an even amount of illumination.

**GENERATORS**—Are machines designed to transform mechanical power into electricity.

**GILDING**—A superficial coating of gold or covering it with some material to give it a golden coloring.

**GINGHAM**—Is a yarn-dyed fabric woven in checks, plaids, stripes or plain colors.

**GLAZE**—Is a mixture of feldspar and other ingredients, which is used to cover the surface of the pottery.

**GLASS**—A clear transparent material made up principally of silica, potash, lime and other incidental elements. Referred to as clear, crystal, flint.

**GOOSENECK**—A curved pipe form, sometimes flexible, sometimes rigid.

**GRAIN**—The term used to indicate the outer or hair side of the hide or skin when it is split into more than two thicknesses. It is the direction of the long fibers of lumber.

**GRAY CARVING**—Grinding ornamentation on the reverse side of glass to be viewed from the front. These surfaces are left gray-unpolished.

**GROSGRAIN**—Meaning "coarse grain" is a firm, stiff, closely woven corded fabric.

**GROUND**—Is the connection made in grounding a circuit.

**HARDWOOD**—Is the lumber gotten from a tree whose cell walls are thicker and more tightly packed.

**HIGH RELIEF**—The projection of ornamentation from its background for half or more than half of its natural circumference.

**HOMESPUN**—Is a loose, rough fabric made of coarse woolen fibers. It is similar to tweed in general character.

**HORSE POWER**—A unit of power equal to 550 foot-pounds of work per second, the power which a horse exerts in pulling, equal to ¾ of a kilowatt or 750 watts.

**HUE**—The quality of a color which identifies it as red, blue, green, yellow, etc.

**IGNEOUS ROCK**—Rock originally formed by hot, molten lavas—affectionately known as fire rocklike granite.

**IMPREGNATED CLOTH**—Cloth permeated or saturated with another material to add new desirable properties.

**INCANDESCENT**—Light which is derived from a filament made luminous by heat.

**INDIRECT LIGHT**—Light which reaches its objective in an indirect route from its source as from an intervening reflecting surface.

**INFRA-RED**—The color whose long wave-length is just below the line of visibility. It is within the area of heat generation.

**INSULATORS**—Are those materials which offer almost total resistance to the flow of current.

**INTAGLIO**—Incising ornamentation below the surface of the material so that an impression of relief imagery is gotten.

**INTENSITY**—The point of saturation of pure hue contained in a color, sometimes referred to as chroma.

**JACQUARD**—Is the technique of reproducing complicated pictures on all cloths using the Jacquard loom to do so.

**JASPE**—Meaning streaked or striped is a faint, broken striped effect, usually woven from printed yarns.

**KAPOK**—Is the trade name for a colorfast fabric made of artificial silk.

**KEENE CEMENT**—A form of spent plaster of paris which results in a harder material, once cast.

**KEYLESS**—A fixture which has no switch on the unit itself.

**KEY LIGHT**—The average degree of general illumination such as high or low.

**KILOWATT**—Equals 1000 watts (1½) horsepower.

**KILOWATT HOURS**—Is the commercial measure of kilowatts used X hours during which it is used.

**LAMINATION**—The process of bonding together superimposed layers of paper, wood, fabric, resinoid on a body material.

**LAMP**—The mechanism which creates the illuminating waves. It is sometimes used to designate the entire fixture used with the lamp.

**LAPIDARY**—The art of cutting or engraving upon stone, precious or otherwise.

**LENS**—A kind of transparent substance used to change the direction of rays of light to form an image within a particular focus.

**LINE DROP**—Is the loss of voltage which is used in forcing the current through the wire toward its destination. The greater the distance, the greater is the line drop.

**LISLE FINISH**—Is a process by which the short, projecting fibers are removed from fine-grade cotton yarns by running them over gas flames.

**LOADING or WEIGHTING**—Is the addition of any substance to increase the weight of a fabric.

**LOUVRES**—A slatted arrangement of panels to permit openings for light or ventilation.

**LUSTERING**—Is a finishing process which produces a luster on cloth by means of heat and pressure.

**MARQUETRY**—A method of decorating wood with small pieces of cut-outs matched like a jig-saw puzzle to cover the surface.

**MERCERIZING**—Cotton fabrics or fibers treated with caustic alkali making it more receptive to dyes, often making it silkier.

**METALLIC CLOTH**—Is a decorative fabric used mainly for trimming and made of metal filling with cotton warp. These filling yarns are produced by winding a strip of tinsel around cotton yarn.

**METAMORPHIC ROCK**—Igneous or sedimentary rock which has been altered by heat, pressure or chemical action like marble.

**MICA**—One of the mineral silicates which readily separate into very thin sheets. The transparent form is commonly called isinglass.

**MINUS**—(—) Is the point toward which electrical current will flow. (Cathode.)

**MODELING**—A technique of shaping materials by pressing or molding it as with a soft material.

**MOGUL SOCKET**—A socket of larger diameter usually used with commercial lamps.

**MOIRE**—Meaning "watered" is a finish on silk, cotton, rayon or other plain weave fabrics which are often corded. This is done by engraved rollers passing over the surface, flattening it with heat and pressure and at intervals leaving the natural roundness in contrast.

**MOTIF**—Is the controlling idea or leading feature of a design.

**MOTORS**—Are machines made to convert electrical power into mechanical power.

**MULTIPLE CIRCUIT**—Is another name for a parallel circuit.

**MUSLIN**—Named after the ancient city of Mosul where it was first made; is a firm, plain white strong heavy cotton fabric.

**NAP**—Unlike pile, is the fuzzy appearance produced by raising the fibers of the cloth as in flannel.

**NET**—Is a mesh-weave cloth which may leave a variety of shaped openings.

**NOVELTY FABRICS**—Cover the large class of materials made to meet a style demand or special need. They have not become staple.

**NYLON PLASTICS**—A synthetic material derived from coal, air and water which can be produced in many forms like thread, sheets, etc.

**OHMS**—Are the units of "friction" (resistance) measured which a conductor offers to a current. Some conductors offer more, some less. Hence they are called poor or good electrical conductors.

**OPAL GLASS**—A white or milky-white glass with a high light diffusing property.

**OPAQUE**—A surface or material impervious to light.

**OUTLET**—An electrical fitting at which the wires terminate for further connection.

**OVERLOAD**—Is an excessive load beyond the regular limit load of line or a piece of apparatus.

**PAINTED FABRICS**—Are colored free-hand in individual or exclusive pattern or picture.

**PARALLEL CIRCUIT**—Is that course which electricity must flow when pieces of electrical apparatus are connected side by side.

**PATINA**—A film or coloring formed on metal by age, exposure or chemical treatment.

**PARCHMENT**—An animal skin, formerly only of sheepskin, now substitute by others.

**PHENOLIC PLASTIC**—One of the thermosetting resins gotten by reaction of phenol with an aldehyde.

**PIERCING**—The process of perforating and removing parts of the material to create a design.

**PILE**—Is the surface of fabric made of upright ends resembling fur.

**PLAID**—Is a box-shaped design usually woven of dyed yarn though sometimes printed afterward.

**PLAIN WEAVE**—Is the simplest of the fundamental weaves often called "tabby" weave.

**PLASTER OF PARIS**—Powdered gypsum rock which when mixed with water forms a plastic mass that hardens.

**PLATING**—A thin coating of metal over some material usually applied by an electrical process.

**PLUG**—A pronged fitting for making an electrical connection by inserting it into a receptacle.

**PLUS**—(+) Is the point from which current flows—plus to minus. (Anode.)

**POLKA DOT**—Is an all-over pattern of round surface dots of any size embroidered, printed or flocked on to the surface of a fabric.

**PYROGRAPHY**—The art of producing pictures or designs on wood, leather or other such material by burning with hot instruments.

**PORCELAIN**—Is another term for China.

**POTTERY**—Is the resultant articles composed of clay and hardened by heat.

**POWER (in watts)**—Used up by any part of a circuit—the product of the current which flows through THAT PART of the circuit X the voltage in JUST THAT SAME PART of the circuit.

**PRESSURE**—Is that factor which causes to flow and not remain static.

**PRINT**—Is the general term referring to printed cotton fabrics. Cretonne, chintz and grandmother cloth are often called "prints."

**PUNCHING**—To perforate a mark or design by striking the material with a sharp tool so imprinted.

**QUARTZ**—A mineral, usually a variety of silicon oxide, which is crystalline in appearance when pure and often used for gems as is amethyst or for larger pieces made of rock-crystal.

**RAMIE**—Sometimes called "China grass," is a fabric made of the fibers of Oriental plant stalks which resemble flax.

**RAYON**—Is a fabric made of cellulose fibers converted from wood pulp or cotton linters which will vary in its properties depending upon the process used to make it.

**REPOUSSE**—Ornamentation formed in relief from the reverse side.

**RHYTHM**—The smoothness of eye-movement or attention offered by the parts of a design to create the gracefulness of the whole.

**RIB**—Is a ridge or cord effect in woven fabric made by heavy filling yarn.

**RIVETING**—The process of uniting two or more pieces by passing a shank through a hole in each piece then pressing or beating down the plain end to make a second head.

**SANFORIZING**—Is a pal nted process that prevents the shrinkage of washable fabrics.

**SATIN**—Is the name of a basic weave which looks like a broken twill. It usually has a high glossy finish.

**SCONCE**—A type of wall bracket consisting of one or more candlesticks.

**SEDIMENTARY ROCK**—Rock laid down by water, wind or results of organic deposits like limestone or sandstone.

SELVEDGE or SELVAGE—Is the finished edge on a woven or knitted fabric.

SERIES CIRCUIT—Is the course through which electricity must pass when pieces of electrical apparatus are connected in tandem.

SHADOW or WARP PRINT—Is the faint or shadowy design gotten by printing it on the warp and weaving over it with plain filling. It is reversible.

SHORT CIRCUIT—A circuit usually made through a part having a lower resistance than the rest and resulting in burning out the circuit fuse.

SHUNT—Is the means used to supply another path for an electrical current.

SILK SCREEN—Imprinting designs on materials by means of using silk as a stencil.

SIZING—Is a finishing process in which yarn and cloth are treated with stiffening substances to give strength, stiffness and smoothness to it.

SKIVED—To shave or pare leather on the reverse side causing it to become thinner.

SOCKET—The part of the fixture which serves as the holder for the electrical connection.

SOFTWOOD—Is applied to lumber made from trees which have thin cells and more uniform in size.

SOLDERING—The method of joining metallic surfaces using an alloy which melts readily at low temperatures.

SPECIFIC LIGHT—Light designed to reach and illuminate a definite area in a room.

SPECTRUM—The visible range of colors extending from the shortest to the longest wave length. Its best known example is the rainbow.

SPLICE—A joining or junction of wires according to safety regulations.

SPOTLIGHT—A concentrated area of illumination to such high key that it is accented against its surroundings.

STAMPING—To forcibly impress or indent a mark or decoration with a stamp, a cut or a die.

STENCIL—A method of making reproductions of pictures, etc., by means of blocking off designated areas with a mask and forcing pigment through the pierced areas.

STORAGE BATTERY—A series of connected electro-chemical cells used to generate electrical energy. May be recharged by reversing the direction of the flow of current.

STYRENE PLASTICS—A plastic material of the unsaturated hydrocarbon family (cinnamic acid) used to make polystyrene plastic (thermoplast).

SWITCH—A device used to control the flow of electricity into the fixture.

TANNING—Process of preparing a skin and making leather out of it.

TAPA CLOTH—Is made without spinning or weaving. It is made by beating flat the inner bark of certain tropical trees in the South Sea Islands to resemble cloth. Usually decorated with batik prints.

TERMINALS—Are the points to and from which current passes through a piece of electrical apparatus.

TEXTURE—Is the surface effect.

THERMOPLAST—A synthetic resinoid material which has the property of becoming soft under application of heat and rigid at normal temperatures no matter how often it is repeated.

THERMOSET—A synthetic resin which has the property of becoming permanently rigid by applying heat which affects a chemical change.

TIE DYE—Is a hand method of producing patterns on cloth when it is dipped in a dye-bath after portions of it has been tied or knotted firmly to create dye-resist areas.

TINNED—To cover a metal with a thin coat of soft solder in preparation for a permanent joint.

TINSEL—Is a synthetic metal filament wound around cotton or silk yarn and used in metal cloth or brocades in imitation of the historic "cloth of gold."

TOILE de JOUY—Is a pictorial print on cotton, usually one color on a light ground, after the manner of the 18th and early 19th Century French prints made at Jouy.

TONE (Value)—The white and black modification of a color. The dark or light quality inherent in a color.

TRANSFORMER—An apparatus used to change electric current from high to low (step-down) or from low to high (step-up) without changing the current energy. Sometimes used interchangeably with a converter.

TWILL—Is a fundamental weave usually recognized by its formed lines running diagonally.

ULTRA-VIOLET—The range of colors beyond the visible short-wave-lengths at the violet end.

UNDERWRITERS' CODE—A set of standards decided on by the union of Insurance Companies which are the minimum requirements for safety.

UNION—Is the term applied to fabrics which combine cotton warp with linen filling or cotton with wool filling.

VELLUM—A fine grade of translucent goatskin, resembling parchment.

VENEER—A thin layer of special material overlayed on some kind of a cove to improve it.

VINYL RESIN PLASTIC—A synthetic material of the thermoplastic group formed by the polymerizing of a vinyl compound.

VOLTAGE—Is the measure of pressure against resistance across two points in a line. It is the product of the amperes X the ohms (unit of resistance measure) or watts divided by amperes.

WARP—Is the set of yarn or threads which runs lengthwise in a piece of woven cloth.

WATT—Is a small unit of electric power; power in watts = volts X amperes.

WAVE LENGTH—The distance between corresponding points on any two consecutive electric waves.

WEAVE—Is to interlace warp threads with filling yarn to form cloth.

WEFT—Is another term for filling or woof.

WEIGHTED SILK—Is gotten when metallic salts are added to the silk.

WELDING—The process of uniting metallic parts by heating the surfaces of the joining parts until melted and allowing the metals to flow together then cool to hardness.

WIRING—To connect the various parts of an electrical circuit with wire conductors.

WOOF—See Weft.

YARN—Is a continuous strand of spun fiber used for weaving or knitting. Used interchangeably with thread although thread is used for sewing and not weaving.

# Sources of Supplies

Wherever possible, first try your local shops, supply companies, offices of national distributors and the chain store branches. If unavailable, then inquire of your nearest listing below. State your request clearly and fully to insure the most satisfying results in return.

**ABRASIVES:**
Armour Sandpaper Works, *Chicago, Ill.*

Behr-Manning Co., *Troy, N. Y.*

**ADHESIVES:**
Ambroid Co., *Boston 10, Mass.*
Bakelite Corp., *New York 17, N. Y.*
Casein Co. of America, *New York, N. Y.*
Catalin Corp., *New York, N. Y.*
M. Ewing Fox Co., *New York, N. Y.*
Franklin Glue Co., *Columbus 15, Ohio*
Furane Plastics & Chemical Co.
 *Los Angeles, Cal.*

Heresite & Chemical Co.
 *Manitowoc, Wisc.*
LePage's, Inc., *Gloucester, Mass.*
Monite Waterproof Glue Co.
 *Minneapolis 11, Minn.*
National Adhesives, *New York 16, N. Y.*
Pennsylvania Coal Products Co.
 *Petrolia, Pa.*
U. S. Plywood Corp., *New York 18, N. Y.*

**ART MATERIALS:**
**(Paints, Brushes, Inks, etc.)**
American Crayon Co., *New York 20, N. Y.*
Milton Bradley, *New York, N. Y.*
Devoe & Reynolds Co., Inc.
 *New York 17, N. Y.*

Higgins Ink Co., *Brooklyn 15, N. Y.*
C. Howard Hunt Pen Co., *Camden, N. J.*
Floquill, Inc., *New York, N. Y.*

**BATTERIES:**
General Dry Batteries, Inc.
 *Cleveland 7, Ohio*

Ray-O-Vac Co., *Madison 3, Wisc.*
Sterling Battery Co., *New York 17, N. Y.*

**CERAMICS & SUPPLIES:**
Amaco, *New York 20, N. Y.*

B. F. Drakenfield & Co.
 *New York 17, N. Y.*

**ELECTRICAL PARTS:**
**(Lamps, Wires, Bases, Plugs, Sockets, Shades, etc.)**
American Lava Corp.
 *Chattanooga 5, Tenn.*
Angelo Brothers, *Philadelphia 45, Pa.*
Associated Manufacturing Co.
 *San Francisco 7, Calif.*
Louis G. Berman Co., *Chicago 23, Ill.*
Chicago Screw Co., *Bellwood, Ill.*
The Finial House, Inc., *New York 10, N. Y.*
General Electric Co., *New York 16, N. Y.*
Gyro Lamp & Shade Co., *Chicago 40, Ill.*
Jay Bee Lamp Parts, Inc.
 *New York 17, N. Y.*
Leviton Mfg. Co.
 *Bklyn. 22, N. Y.; Chicago 6, Ill.;
 Los Angeles 12, Calif.*

Clyde W. Lint, *Chicago 7, Ill.*
Metalart Lamp Mounting Co.
 *Brooklyn 12, N. Y.*
Metomic Corp., *Chicago 23, Ill.*
Noma Electric Corp., Inc.
 *New York 11, N. Y.*
North American Electric Lamp Co.
 *St. Louis 6, Mo.*
Royal Electric Co., Inc., *Pawtucket, R. I.*
Harry Sanders Co., *Chicago 6, Ill.*
Standard Arms Works
 *New York 13, N. Y.*
United Pipe & Nipple Corp.
 *Chicago 8, Ill.*
Wheeler Manufacturing Co.
 *Wheeler, Wisc.*

## FABRICS:

Apex Coated Fabric Co.
  *New York 10, N. Y.*
American Felt Company, *Glenville, Conn.*
American Velour Mills Co., Inc.
  *Bound Brook, N. J.*
Athol Manufacturing Co., *Athol, Mass.*
The Bolta Company, *Lawrence, Mass.*
Columbus Coated Fabrics Co.
  *Columbus, Ohio*

Henrose, *New York 22, N. Y.;*
  *Chicago, Ill.; Dallas, Tex.;*
  *Washington, D. C.*
Masland Duraleather Co.
  *Philadelphia, Pa.*
Spaulding Fibre Co., *Tonawanda, N. Y.*
Switzer Brothers, Inc., *Cleveland, Ohio*
Textileather Corp., *Toledo, Ohio*

## FABRICS and LEATHER:

Allied Products, *Baltimore 2, Md.*
Consolidated Trimming Co.,
  *New York 10, N. Y.*
Dazian's, Inc., *New York 22, N. Y.*
John Duer & Sons, Inc., *Baltimore, Md.*
Haeckel Weaves, *Los Angeles, Calif.*
S. M. Hexter Co.
  *Cleveland 14, Ohio; New York 22, N. Y.*

Maharam Fabric Corp.
  *New York 22, N. Y.*
E. L. Mansure Co., *Chicago, Ill.*
Snapco Manufacturing Corp.
  *Bloomfield, N. J.*
Standard Trimming Corp.
  *New York 22, N. Y.*

## GENERAL SUPPLIES & KITS:

American Handicraft Co.
  *East Orange, N. J.*
Craft Service, *Rochester 7, N. Y.*
Design Craft Products, *Chicago, Ill.*
Griffin Craft Supplies, *Oakland 9, Calif.*
Kit Kraft, *Hollywood 46, Calif.*

J. C. Larson Co., *Chicago 24, Ill.*
Russo Handicraft Supplies
  *Los Angeles 12, Calif.*
Universal Handicraft Co.
  *New York 17, N. Y.*
Magnus Brush & Craft Material Co.
  *New York 13, N. Y.*

## GLASS:

American Window Glass Co., *Atlanta;*
  *Boston; Chicago; Detroit; New York;*
  *St. Louis; San Francisco; Los Angeles;*
  *Portland; Salt Lake City; Seattle; and*
  *Toronto, Can.*
Glass & Wire Supply Co.
  *New York 7, N. Y.*
Hazel-Atlas Glass Co., *New York 12, N. Y.*

Libby-Owen-Ford Company, *Toledo, Ohio*
Master Glass Company
  *Clarksburg, W. Va.*
Mississippi Glass Company, *New York;*
  *St. Louis; Chicago; Fullerton (Calif.)*
Pittsburgh Plate Glass Co.
  *Pittsburgh, Pa.*

## LAMP KITS:

Glass & Wire Supply Co.
  *New York 7, N. Y.*

No. American Electric Lamp Co.
  *St. Louis 6, Mo.*

## LEATHER:

Hatton Leather Co.
  *Grand Haven, Mich.*
A. C. Lawrence Leather Co.
  *Peabody, Mass.*
Leathercraft Corporation
  *New York 10, N. Y.*

L. Lefkowitz & Bro., Inc.
  *New Brunswick, N. J.*
Tandy Leather Company
  *Fort Worth, Texas*

## LUMBER and WOODS:

Anderson-Tully Co., *Memphis 1, Tenn.*
Caddo River Lumber Co.
  *Kansas City, Mo.*
Craftsman Wood Service Co.
  *Chicago 8, Ill.*

Long Bell Lumber Co.
  *Longview, Wash.*
Maine Lumber Products Corp.
  *Old Town, Maine*
Red River Lumber Co., *Westwood, Calif.*

Frost Lumber Industries Inc.
*Shreveport, La.*

U. S. Plywood Corp., *New York 19, N. Y.*

**METALS:**
Allegheny Steel & Brass Corp.
*Chicago 51, Ill.*
Cornell Manufacturing Co.
*Long Island City 1, N. Y.*
Feldman Bros. Brass Co.
*New York 13, N. Y.*
Metropolis Metal Spinning & Stamping
Co., Inc., *New York, N. Y.*

Ornamental Tube Co., *Norton, Mass.*
Reliable Pipe & Nipple Works Co.
*Brooklyn, N. Y.*
Standard Arms Works, *New York 13, N. Y.*
Universal Brass Turning Co.
*Bronx 51, N. Y.*

**NOVELTIES:**
**(for Lamps)**
Lipper & Mann, *New York 10, N. Y.*

**PAPER:**
Commercial Paper Co.
*Philadelphia 6, Pa.*

Shopsin Paper Co., *New York 14, N. Y.*

**PLASTICS:**
American Plastics Corp.
*New York 17, N .Y.*
Cadillac Plastics Co., *Detroit 2, Mich.*
Carmen-Broson Co., *Mount Vernon, N. Y.*
The Castolite Co., *Woodstock, Ill.*
D. W. Cope Plastics
*St. Louis 21, Mo.*
Flexcraft Industries, *New York 56, N. Y.*

Kosto Hobby Craft Plastics Co.
*Washington 7, D. C.*
The Lockrey Co., *College Point 3, N. Y.*
Plasticast Co., *Chicago 6, Ill.*
Plastic Parts & Sales Co.
*St. Louis 10, Mo.*
Plastic Products Co., *Salt Lake City, Utah*
Plastic Supply Co., *St. Louis 7, Mo.*
Polyplastex United, Inc., *New York, N. Y.*

**SPRAYERS:**
Blasto Spray Gun Mfg. Co.
*Los Angeles 47, Calif.*
DeVilbiss Co., *Toledo 1, Ohio*
Ideal Air Brush Mfg. Co., *New York, N. Y.*

Paasche Airbrush Co., *Chicago, Ill.*
Wold Air Brush Mfg. Co.
*Los Angeles 47, Calif.*

**STONE, MARBLE,**
**PLASTER, ETC.:**
U. S. Gypsum Corp., *New York, N. Y.*

**TOOLS:**
Atlas Press Co., *Kalamazoo 3, Mich.*
Brodhead-Garrett Co., *Cleveland 5, Ohio*
Burgess Battery Co., *Chicago 1, Ill.*
Delta Tool Div. (Rockwell Mfg. Co.)
*Milwaukee 1, Wisc.*
William Dixon, Inc., *Newark 1, N. J.*

Heller Bros., *Newark 4, N. J.*
Patterson Bros., *New York 7, N. Y.*
Richter Tool Co., *New York 17, N. Y.*
Stanley Tools, *New Britain, Conn.*
X-Acto Crescent Products Co.
*New York 16, N. Y.*

**WIRE PARTS and FORMS:**
Continental Steel Corp., *Kokomo, Ind.*
Merrill Mfg. Corp., *Merrill, Wisc.*
Seneca Wire & Mfg. Co., *Fostoria, Ohio*

Edwin B. Stimpson Co.
*Brooklyn 5, N. Y.*
Wilson Steel & Wire Co., *Chicago, Ill.*

CPSIA information can be obtained at www.ICGtesting.com
Printed in the USA
BVOW080638111012

302639BV00002B/80/P